# How to overcome fear of driving

# How to overcome fear of driving

## The road to driving confidence

Joanne Mallon

NELL JAMES PUBLISHERS

*Published by* Nell James Publishers
www.nelljames.co.uk
info@nelljames.co.uk

*British Library Cataloguing-in-Publication Data*
A catalogue record for this book is available from the British Library.

ISBN 978-0-9567024-6-3

First published 2012.

The Publisher has no responsibility for the persistence or accuracy of URLs for external or any third-party internet websites referred to in this book, and does not guarantee that any content on such websites is, or will remain, accurate or appropriate.

*Note:* The advice and information included in this book is published in good faith. However, the Publisher and author assume no responsibility or liability for any loss, injury or expense incurred as a result of relying on the information stated. Please check with the relevant persons and authorities regarding any legal and medical issues.

Printed in Great Britain.

This book is dedicated to my family,
my best travelling companions in every situation:
John Higgs, Lia Higgs and Isaac Higgs.

# Contents

Introduction ........................................................................... 1

1. What is driving anxiety? Am I the only one?........................ 7

2. Fear of motorways and other situations.............................. 23

3. Why drive? What's so great about driving anyway?............. 35

4. Stress relief: how to deal with driving-related stress............. 43

5. First steps to regaining your driving confidence................... 65

6. Dealing with anxiety and panic attacks................................ 89

7. Therapy: what to expect and how it can help..................... 113

8. Success stories: people who've overcome fear of driving 127

Useful contacts and other resources ..................................... 137

Index...................................................................................... 143

# Introduction

This is a book for anyone experiencing any degree of fear of driving – whether you don't drive at all and can barely look at a car; or if you drive sporadically, or even every day but still don't like doing so. You may feel that you have a phobia, a deeply held fear or simply a niggling sense of unease that you want to conquer. This is a book for anyone who wants to step away from fear of driving and towards becoming a confident driver instead.

So thank you for reading this book. Thank you for taking the first steps down your road to driving confidence. It may prove to be a long road, but I am there with you all the way. I know you can get there because I've travelled this road myself. I know that it is a tough one, but I also know that it's not an impossible one. We can get there together.

In this book we're going to take a journey through, and away from, fear of driving. We'll be looking at why it happens, what the causes are and how you can overcome it.

There will be practical exercises you can do in the comfort of your own home, before you even set foot in a car (so don't worry that I'm going to send you zooming off down the motorway before you're ready). Some of these involve writing things down, so it's probably a good idea to grab a notebook and a pen now.

There will be tips for things you can do whilst you're actually driving, to support yourself and make the experience easier and (eventually) one you can enjoy. We'll also look at what you can do if you feel yourself starting to have a panic attack whilst you're driving.

We'll be hearing from many people who feel like you and want to share their stories – you'll be surprised at just how widespread fear of driving seems to be. And we'll be taking inspiration from people who used to be scared to drive, but who overcame that fear and have moved on from it.

And that's why I've written this book – because I overcame fear of driving and I want to help you to do the same. If I've done it and other people have done it, you can do it too.

In the last year I drove on some fantastic journeys – work assignments in outlying places that I would have otherwise had to turn down; travelling through wild mountains and amazing scenery on holiday; dashing to a remote hospital so I could be a birth partner and witness the safe delivery of my friend's baby. None of this would have been possible had I not overcome my fear of driving. It kept me off the road and dictated my life for seven years, but not any more.

Though I passed my driving test at the first attempt at age 18, it's fair to say that I was never a particularly confident driver. And yet I did it. I forced myself to drive. Whilst living in London in my twenties, I got a highly stressful job 200 miles north of there and used to take weekly trips up and down the motorway. I bought my first car especially for this trip. It was an old style black Mini, a bit of a clapped out banger, but I liked it.

One day I was out driving in heavy traffic in the centre of London, and as I put my foot on the brake pedal, it simply floated to the floor without the brakes engaging or the car stopping. I steered it over to the side and into a housing estate where it came to a natural halt. How we never hit another car, or a person, I'll never know.

In the later stages of my driving phobia, this incident was to come back to haunt me many times – I would have flashbacks and visions of what might have been. What if the brakes had failed at a pedestrian crossing? What if I had run over a child because the car wouldn't stop? The fact that neither of these scenarios actually happened didn't matter – I still felt the fear and the stress of what might have been.

With brand new brakes and a host of other repairs, my old banger had a new lease of life. But I never felt entirely comfortable in it again.

Soon after that I became pregnant with my first child. I was back working full time in London, so had less need of the car. Plus I could barely fit my baby bump behind the Mini's steering wheel. So I sold it, to a new teenage driver who zoomed off up the road.

After our daughter was born, my partner and I decided that we needed a car after all to cart about all the paraphernalia that a baby accrues. So another old banger it was. But this time my partner bought it, and although technically it was our car, I rarely sat in the driver's seat. And the less I did it, the less I wanted to. The less I believed that I could do it, safely.

And then there was the baby to consider. Injuring yourself in a car is one thing – but injuring the precious child you've just given birth to? Every mother's worst nightmare.

There was another incident, stretching back through the years, which returned to haunt me and reinforce my belief that a car was a dangerous place to be.

When I was four, I attended a day nursery. I guess nurseries in the 1970's were very different places to how they are today, judging by what happened when I was in their care. One day, one of the children at the nursery was off sick with chicken pox. The nursery staff went to visit, taking some of the children with them. I remember we were all lined up, half a dozen little people packed along the back seat, and I was next to the car door.

When we stopped at our classmate's house, the nursery worker was at the door talking to the mum, but our friend crept out to see us. I opened the car door to talk to her, then she slipped away and we shut the door before driving off. As far as I remember, the adults hadn't seen this happening, and so didn't know that the door had been opened. Only, being four years old, I didn't shut the door very well.

Then I remember bouncing from side to side with my friends as we all sang a song. Back and forth we bounced – until the badly closed door popped open and I fell out on to the road, in the midst of a dual carriageway.

Though it's nearly 40 years ago, I can still remember it clear as today. Rolling over and over again on the concrete, seeing the tyres of cars as they drove towards me. I remember a brown Mini in particular, seeing the underside of its wheels bearing down on me every time I rolled around. And yet somehow I managed to roll over on to the hard shoulder and escaped from this with barely a scratch.

It was a terrifying incident, but I was a little girl and you would hope that I could get over this incident and forget about it easily. For many years I did, but it must have buried down within my subconscious, until it eventually came back to haunt me.

Without warning, fear of driving struck like a demon and before I knew it I could barely look at a car. And that's how it was for seven years. And yet here we are today, when I can and do choose to drive for pleasure.

It's only many years on, having researched the subject that I realise that all of these incidents put together mean that I was a textbook case for potential driving phobia. It would have been more of a wonder if I hadn't developed it.

So in this book I have drawn on the experiences of many people. First of all there's my own experience – and having felt the full terror of driving, including panic attacks on the road, yet having overcome this fear, I fully believe that you can do it too. I believe in you. You may be carrying this fear, but it is not carrying you, and one day you will put it down and walk away from it. Or drive away from it, if you want to.

I would like to thank the professionals working in this field who have contributed expert advice and help. You'll find their contact details in the back of the book – please do seek them out. They know what they're doing, and they can help.

And lastly I would like to acknowledge the people who've experienced fear of driving and shared their stories, both in this book and elsewhere. Some are proud that they have overcome it. Others are very matter of fact about it, have found a way to accept it and simply treat it, like a scar, as part of who they are. Others are deeply ashamed of feeling like this.

But they're all heroes really, because they're part of the evidence that this is a massive phenomenon. We are everywhere. As I was researching this book and talking to people, I could pretty much guarantee that if I was in a group of three people or more then at least one of them would know someone who was afraid to drive, or be a reluctant driver themselves.

Many people who are scared to drive said to me 'I thought I was the only one' – so if you only take away one message from this book, know this: you're not alone, you are one of many. Those people that you see on the roads, whom you assume must be ultra-confident drivers? Well, often they're not. Some of them are just as scared as you. This fear is everywhere. It is no respecter of age or social status. From teens taking their first tentative trips behind the wheel to retirees who's been driving without problems their whole life – a fear of driving is a shadow that can fall on anybody. But equally, it's a shadow you can move away from.

The aim of this book is to help you understand your fear and what is going on in your mind and body when you feel the way you do and give you practical strategies to deal with this fear. Because ultimately, it's not about the driving at all – it's about living your life as a victim of fear. You deserve better than that. Your journey is a happier one than that.

**Joanne Mallon**
www.JoannetheCoach.com
info@joannemallon.com
Twitter @joannemallon

# 1. What is driving anxiety? Am I the only one?

In this chapter we're taking an overview of driving anxiety as a whole to help you understand what's really going on when people feel scared to drive. We'll also hear from a variety of people who have experienced driving phobia, and experts who have worked with clients to help them overcome it.

The aim of this chapter is to help you demystify these feelings by examining their roots. Once you know where you're coming from, it's easier to find a way out.

Rather than seeing this fear as an unavoidable part of your personality, try to see it as something you can examine in an objective way – like an object in the room, rather than an intrinsic part of you. This is an important first step in disengaging from the fear (note that we're saying 'the fear' rather than 'my' or 'your fear': you don't own it and it's not a permanent part of you).

You may find it helpful to read this chapter with a notebook or journal and pen at hand, to jot down any similarities you find between what's described here, and your own experience.

So in this chapter we're asking:

- Where does fear of driving come from? What are the common causes or contributing factors?
- How does it start?
- Why do some people and not others become afraid to drive?

## What is driving phobia?

At its simplest – driving phobia is described as a condition in which a person exhibits high levels of anxiety at the prospect of driving, or during driving. However, this doesn't mean that people with fear of driving necessarily stop doing it. Some people express quite a high degree of fear around driving, even though they do it every day. For some, this fear is so great that they abandon driving altogether, whilst others stick to limited driving only in situations where they feel safe.

And it's important to note that avoiding driving completely doesn't mean that the fear will go away – in fact there's a chance it may increase. Even if you have decided that driving is not for you, there will still be times when you have to be a passenger in someone else's car, or travel on the roads via public transport, with the evidence of your fear all around you. So deciding to deal with these feelings by not driving doesn't really deal with them at all, and they can still increase.

Dr David Kraft is a psychotherapist with a special interest in phobic anxiety and driving anxiety. He points out that there are secondary gains to be had from this condition:

> 'People can gain rewards from not driving – they're able to have a drink, they don't have to pay road tax and can avoid the responsibilities that go with running a car. Sometimes a phobia can give you something good, as by avoiding confronting your fears you may also avoid having to be grown up. At the centre of it all is a fear of lack of control.'
> www.londonhypnotherapyuk.com

**A phobia that dare not speak its name – because it hasn't got one**
There is no officially recognised medical word for driving phobia. Whilst fear of spiders can command the grand-sounding name of Arachnophobia, fear of driving has no such official title. It's sometimes called Hodophobia, which is the term for a more general fear of travel – coming from the Greek word 'hodos' meaning path or road, the term is taken to mean fear of travelling by road. But that's not quite the same as fear of driving, is it?

The term Amaxophobia is also applied to a fear of travelling by vehicle (planes and trains as well as cars), but again it's more about being driven than doing the driving yourself.

You might think that Autophobia would suit pretty well, but that's already been claimed as the word for a fear of being alone. Perhaps we should lay claim to Autoautophobia – fear of being alone in a car. And whilst you might think 'What's in a name?' little things like this do make a difference.

There's also very little official research into driving phobia, though some smaller studies have emerged in recent years. So if the medical establishment can't even be bothered to name or look into how you're feeling, it's no surprise that sufferers end up feeling adrift and ignored. You might even assume that it's a very uncommon and unusual phobia to have. Not so at all.

*The Spanish experience*

A survey in Spain undertaken by the Mapfre Foundation's Institute for Road Safety in 2011 found that 8.5 million people in Spain – that's 33% of all those who have a driving license – admitted to being scared of driving in certain circumstances. Those circumstances included bad weather, heavy traffic, driving at night and journeys they've never done before. So, quite a lot, really.

A total of 1.5 million Spanish people (six per cent of the total number of drivers) declared they were afraid to drive at all.

The study found that twice as many women as men admitted to having a fear of driving, with the vast majority of these being people over 40 who needed to drive sporadically rather than regularly, and who had either witnessed or been involved in a serious traffic accident.

Men who admitted to this fear were found to be more likely to be older (age 60 and above), and in these cases it was more likely to be related to other health issues.

**So why do people become afraid to drive?**
Whilst researching this book, four common factors stood out when people told me about the background to their driving phobia. Can you tick any of these boxes?

*1. A parent who was a non driver or an unconfident driver*
Women in particular talked of their mother shrieking or behaving nervously in the car – it's not surprising that that might have an effect if you grew up with it as a role model. Or they had no adult role model to base their own driving on, if one or both parents were a non driver. I think that this factor is particularly interesting if you're a parent now and you're scared to drive. Do you want to pass that on to your child, as it may have been passed on to you?

*2. Experience of any type of car crash*
Either the fear of driving started directly after the incident, or (more commonly) people said they experienced a delayed reaction, i.e. it may not start straight away. Sometimes it takes a further episode of stress (not necessarily to do with driving) to tip a person over into a full blown fear. These car crashes/driving incidents could be minor or severe, or could even be a near miss rather than an actual crash.

*3. A prolonged and high degree of stress*
This seems to be what makes the difference between the person who is involved in a car crash which doesn't develop into a fear, and one who does – the presence of some other form of stress in their lives. It could be some sort of major, life changing incident such as having a baby, divorce, illness or a highly pressured job. So whilst the stress might not be enough of a trigger by itself, partner this with some sort of incident whilst in a car and you have the potential for a fairly major fear.

*4. Stopping driving for a period of time*
Particularly when any of the above applies. People who stopped driving in the immediate aftermath of a crash, or perhaps around

the time of stress or a major life change such as when they had a baby, frequently found it much harder to get going again.

So take a moment now to think about your experience of fear and see if you can trace a line from it to any of the sorts of situations mentioned above. What was going on in your life immediately prior to you starting to feel afraid to drive?

I can pretty much tick every box here – my mother, despite many lessons, has never really driven, doesn't want to and is a nervous passenger; the brakes failed, plus I'd fallen out of a car as a child; I'd had a stressful job and just had a baby; I stopped driving when we sold the car.

Tick, tick, tick, tick. That's one test I've passed with flying colours.

### Expert opinion: phobia triggers aren't just about the driving

Julian Smith runs Ride Drive, a UK-wide specialist company which offers a programme to help people overcome their fear of driving. He feels that whilst a car crash or other incident may be a trigger for the start of a phobia, they are rarely its true cause:

'If someone tells me they had a crash or a specific life event that triggered their phobia, then I always ask them – what else was going on in your life at that time? And there is always some sort of stress also present. It could be re-dundancy, or an acrimonious divorce, something that means they're already tight as a drum nerves-wise, and then something like a minor traffic accident is enough to trigger off something more serious.

For women, I find that having a baby is the most common trigger. You've got all the stress of a major life change, and worrying am I going to be a good enough mum?

With the rise of stress in society, we've seen a corresponding rise in driving phobias. The recession has brought in more work than ever, from men and women – some of my instructors are booked up for weeks on end. People think that they're the only one who's afraid of driving.'
www.ridedrive.co.uk

## Expert opinion: you can overcome this phobia

Hypnotherapist Barbara Ford-Hammond has been working with clients for over 20 years and has seen a variety of reasons that spark off driving phobia:

- Post trauma, i.e. being in a crash regardless of whose fault;
- Witnessing a crash, losing someone through a car accident (in or hit);
- Motorway driving: particularly overtaking or getting caught in middle lane can set off fears. I think people doubt their abilities or misjudge speed;
- Breaking down and feeling unsafe. Or, just generally feeling unsafe;
- People who have been victims to road rage;
- People who have road rage;
- Fear of turning right, or left depending which country;
- Vomiting in a car. Either self or being with someone who has (emetophobia is very common);
- And issues that are not always related but transferred to driving, i.e. claustrophobia, agoraphobia, attacks of vertigo, illness (example diarrhoea, worry of being caught short).

Ford-Hammond has found that women are more likely than men to come forward for help, but when they do seek help, it's usually with a successful outcome:

'If anyone has a fear or phobia that they wish to overcome then they can. It isn't necessary to relive the original cause but it is necessary to heal or change automatic fear or anxiety reactions.

Left unchecked worries can grow. The issues are stored subconsciously and even if a person knows why they have a problem it is the way the mind has stored it or associated it that keeps repeating or switches on the fear response.

The brain cannot detect reality from imagination, hence our ability to be terrified during a film or aroused through a fantasy. Imagining being calm, safe and in control creates new neural pathways and sets up new reactions. If someone expects they'll be stressed or worried they are guaranteeing that outcome.'
www.barbaraford-hammond.com

## Expert opinion: it's a learned fear, so you can unlearn it

Whilst there are a lot of common themes that can lead to driving phobia, it's a recipe with an uncertain outcome, since no two people's fears are exactly the same. Dominic Knight is a Master NLP Practitioner and Hypnotherapist who has a phenomenally successful track record in treating severely phobic cases from his clinic in Harley Street, London. He says that fear of driving is a learned rather than an innate fear, and, because this is the case, it means that you can learn to overcome it:

'There are only two fears that as human beings we are all born with: one is the fear of falling and the other is the fear of loud noises. So the fear of driving is a learned fear and because there was once a time before you ever had the fear it means you are capable of getting back to being free of fear. There is no such thing as an incurable phobia of driving. Though the rate of time it takes for a person to overcome the fear may vary.

The phobia of driving can affect anyone, it triggers either from a specific event such as an accident or it may trigger as a result of accumulating anxieties, which are unrelated to driving. So if you are driving while anxious about work, money or relationships the anxiety actually can associate with driving. So many times when I work with someone they have no conscious recollection of how the fear started, they just felt discomfort then it got worse.'

But Dominic has words of comfort for anyone who thinks that they're just not meant to drive:

'Absolutely everyone who is physically capable of driving is capable of driving well. The problem is that often they don't believe it themselves, and that's the first thing that has to change before they will have any chance of getting confident and comfortable in a car. Unfortunately whilst they are in such a flustered and confused state, their driving is likely to be poor and erratic and therefore they will gather more evidence that it's just something they cannot do.'

Is it more common with men or women, or at particular times in a person's life?

'There is a common misconception that women will be more fearful of driving, but the apprehension is fairly well distributed between the sexes for the reasons above.

The longer you leave mastering the skill the more out of step and at odds you feel with the rest of the "normal" population. This often bruises your confidence, which is often the key skill you need to learn to drive well.'
www.dominicknight.co.uk

**Symptoms**

The symptoms of driving phobia vary from person to person, and depending on the degree of the fear may include:

- Shakiness in the arms or legs;
- Sweating;
- Feeling dizzy;
- Increased heartbeat;
- Altered senses – your hearing or sight may be affected. Extra sound like the car radio or people talking may irritate you more than usual. Or alternatively you may prefer some background noise as a distraction;
- Feeling lightheaded;
- A feeling of unreality and being disconnected from the world around you. Even though you may be on strong, solid ground, you may feel that the road is going to rise up beneath you, or that you're going to tip over the edge;
- A feeling of being out of control of your arms or legs – you may feel that you could swerve without warning, or slam on the breaks or accelerator pedal.

You don't have to be actually driving for any of these symptoms to occur – in fact, you might be nowhere near the car. With a very deep fear, sometimes just the thought or prospect of driving will be enough to trigger a physical response.

But if you are driving and feeling like this, you can see how they're not exactly conducive to safe and happy motoring.


**Fear or driving: is it a male or a female thing?**

The therapists I spoke to said that whilst this fear is very common amongst both sexes, they tended to see more women who had a fear of driving than men. Sometimes men would come to see a professional for another reason, such as stress, and the fact that they were avoiding driving would emerge later in the treatment process.

Whilst I've been interviewing people for this book, it's been very notable that far more women have come forward to speak about it than men. But this doesn't mean that they necessarily suffer from it more – it could simply be that they are happier to speak openly about it. Cognitive Therapist Dan Roberts comments:

'As with all health-related problems, men are far less willing to talk about or seek treatment for their stress. They may be worried about seeming weak or vulnerable, or may not even know they are stressed – they might just feel really irritable and snappy. Women are generally much more in tune with their emotions and inner experience, as well as being far more willing to seek help.'
www.danroberts.com

Dr Rick Norris is Chartered Psychologist, Visiting Consultant at the Manor Hospital Walsall, and author of *Think Yourself Happy – The Simple Six Step Programme to Change Your Life from Within*. He says:

'As far as I am aware there are no specific gender differences in terms of phobias. With regard to driving although I have seen women who have a fear of driving, I have not seen any men. This could be a chance statistic or it could be that men are less open about admitting it.

Another point that might be worth bearing in mind is that it is generally recognised that men's spatial awareness is better than women's. Men find it much easier to parallel park than women and are also much better than women with directions (they are able to identify north south east and west quite accurately without the aid of a compass). Not that this necessarily makes men "better" drivers than women but it might make it a less challenging task for men. Women on the other hand are statistically safer drivers than men with fewer accidents. This may be linked to

the lack of spatial awareness compared to men, which in turn makes them more cautious drivers, and therefore less likely to have accidents.'
www.mindhealthdevelopment.co.uk

Hypnotherapist Sharon Stiles says that although men and women with phobias tend to have the same physical and mental response to the thing they fear, the vast majority of her clients with driving phobia have been women:

> 'As a generalisation, I think men consider it important that they are good drivers. So I think they are less likely to talk about any driving concerns in general conversation as they wouldn't want to "lose face". For some of my older clients, one of the issues was that women weren't really expected to drive, it was what the man did, so it didn't feel natural to them.
>
> One of the factors is people who don't drive very often. Someone who only drives to the shops occasionally or picks the children up from school is more likely to be anxious because they don't have the different driving experiences and the confidence that comes with those.
>
> Another factor is the birth of children. Many parents become more anxious after the birth of their first child because suddenly they have increased responsibility and so they feel they have to be more careful. People who have happily speeded up and down motorways day after day can suddenly become nervous about driving long journeys or in fast traffic. As women tend to be the main carers it is them who tend to be more affected by this.'
> www.sharonstiles.co.uk

### Living with fear of driving

We don't always realise how much the ability to drive affects our lives until we can't do it. So if you are afraid of driving, it may change your choices about where you live, what job you do, your social life, your family life, your relationships – the ripples spread far and wide.

For many people, the ability to drive means freedom and independence, and this phobia can take all that away from you. And this is why it becomes more important than ever not to be beaten and to overcome your phobia. It's about much more than the ability to take a trip in the car – it's about not letting fear rule your life.

*Rebecca's story:*
Rebecca has found that her reluctance to drive is affecting her family and working life:

> 'I am now on maternity leave. I should be driving to young mum groups, or swimming classes with my baby, but daren't. This means I am very isolated. I am already dreading going back to work and am trying to work out ways that I could work from home doing I don't know what, just so I can avoid having to drive.'

Rebecca is typical of many new mums I spoke to, who found that their fear of driving was restricting their life and casting a big shadow of stress over their daily lives.

*SH's story*
SH has always found driving to be a problem, which he traces back to his dad's attitude:

> 'I will not drive "out of my area" much to the amusement of family and friends. My area being about a 20 mile radius of where I live and roads and places I know well. For many years I experienced acute embarrassment at this but as I have got older I don't really care what people think and make a joke of it.
>
> My theory is my Dad is at the bottom of it. I grew up to car journeys where I listened to him criticise everyone

else's driving. Therefore I feel I am one of those "other" drivers who is not driving properly and so inconveniencing others.'

SH has found that this fear has affected his life, as his work choices have been affected by how much driving was involved. Although it's interesting to note that he has found a coping mechanism of sorts in choosing not to care about what other people think and laughing about it all instead.

*Alison's story*
Alison Percival is a 45-year old freelance journalist who has repeatedly attempted to learn to drive, without success:

> 'When I was pregnant in my early 30s, I had a major panic attack with my husband driving and he had to stop the car. My husband gets annoyed that he always has to be the designated driver and that holidays etc are limited.'

Alison's distress at not driving is palpable. She has managed to work her life around it, but it's clear she'd rather not have to do this.

*Geoff's story*
Despite passing his test at an early age, 37-year old Geoff avoids driving as much as possible.

> 'It would be great to overcome this as driving is something I'd like to conquer. It has caused problems as I travel a lot for work and stupidly have "clean driving licence" on my CV. When caught out, I've always refused to hire a car and have only got away with it as taking individual cabs – though expensive – are still less than hiring a car for several days.'

So Geoff's another example of someone who's found a way to work around this, without actually admitting his fear to his workmates (where would we be without taxi drivers?). He shows how a job which involves some driving isn't an absolute no-no for a non-driver – so don't assume that your fear of driving will automatically rule out certain jobs. With creative thinking, you can find a way round anything and not be beaten by fear.

*Lynne's story*
Lynne is a 38-year old mother who finds her fear of driving very distressing. She can tick all the boxes in terms of having a break in driving, combined with major life change and being involved in a traffic incident. It's affected her very deeply:

> 'More than anything I'd like to be able to get in a car and drive. I see people who don't even look as if they can spell their own names hopping into their cars and driving off and yet I'm a reasonably intelligent person who had a decent career and I can't even get into the driver's seat without crying and feeling sick. I just feel like an absolute idiot.'

Lynne expresses what many people with fear of driving told me, and what I felt myself. It's a horrible feeling of powerlessness. But it's not a forever feeling. There is hope for everybody. There is hope for you.

**Expert opinion: it's not just about the driving**
Charles Linden is an anxiety expert and developer of *The Linden Method Program*, which has helped over 140,000 anxious people in over 40 countries deal with panic attacks, phobias and anxiety.

Q. How common do you think fear of driving is? Is it more common with men or women, or at particular times in a person's life?

'Fear of driving is a common symptom of a high anxiety condition and is normally unrelated to driving itself but more with feeling trapped, feeling removed from people or a place of safety or attached to a previous anxiety provoking experience whilst driving.

Fear of driving seems to be more common in women than in men. In men, the most common catalyst for driving anxiety is an underlying high anxiety condition. It is vital that the underlying high anxiety condition is addressed directly.'

Q. But can everyone be cured of driving phobia?

'I think that this depends solely on a person's ability to drive. If a person is an appalling driver and they recognise this, this should be the initial issue to address with some driving skills classes.

If a person is a competent driver but experiences high anxiety whilst behind the wheel, an inappropriate "risk assessment" of the situation by the brain can be at fault. Because the mind is "reading" driving as a risk, far beyond the actual risk present, it then responds with anxiety to "fight or flee" from that risk. In this case, the only solution is to undo the changes that cause the inappropriate anxiety response at their core [...] No amount of "feel the fear and do it anyway" or "exposure therapy" can fix this problem.'
www.charles-linden.com

**So where does that leave us?**
Throughout this book we will look at various aspects of fear of driving and how you might deal with them.

One thing to bear in mind is: the stronger your driving phobia, the less likely it is that you'll be able to overcome it by yourself. Whether you go to see a hypnotherapist, doctor, driving instructor or other professional, it's unlikely that you'll pull yourself out of this hole alone. Yes, some people can and do manage it, and we'll be meeting some of them in each chapter.

The other factor to consider is that whilst it can be overcome, dealing with this issue is not to be rushed, and it is realistic to expect that it will take some time to move on from this particular phobia – a minimum of weeks, more likely months. You're not going to wake up tomorrow, jump into a car and it'll be gone. It just doesn't work like that.

## Success story
*Penny's story: phobic turned hypnotherapist*
Penny Ling overcame her phobia and turned it into something positive as she now works as a hypnotherapist helping others overcome their fear of driving. Penny recalls:

'I used to work at the local newspaper and had the horrible job of painting out the bodies in photos of car crashes for news stories. This was before the days of Photoshop, so you literally were painting them out. This amplified my general anxiety around driving, and I stopped doing it altogether from 1995 to 2001.

When I began training as a hypnotherapist, we were encouraged to tackle our own phobias. Over around three weeks I built up my confidence. Then I had a driving lesson, and the instructor said he never would have thought I'd had a problem. I've been driving ever since. I feel calm and don't panic. Now I look forward to going out in my car, I love it. Now when people come to me as a hypnotherapist for help they know I can understand this fear and how to overcome it.'
www.pennyling.co.uk

# 2. Fear of motorways and other situations

It's clear that there's more to this fear of driving than meets the eye. However, even though the fear itself is very common, some people find that it only asserts itself in certain situations. So they can drive perfectly well on ordinary roads, but go miles out of their way to avoid driving over a bridge, or taking a right hand turn. They may be fine within the comfort zone of their locality, but freeze at the thought of driving somewhere new, particularly if it involves a motorway.

Here we examine common situations that people find scary, and look at why some aspects of driving and not others can become frightening. Once again as we did in Chapter One, the point of doing this, of looking at the fear from the outside, picking it up and examining the different shadows it throws is to help you do the same. I want you to take a step outside your fear and in doing so make it less of 'your' fear and just 'a' fear – a thing that exists but is not inevitable part of you.

The other aim of this chapter is to once again show you that you are not alone with this – take comfort in the fact that it isn't just you, many people feel the same way too.

As we've seen in the first chapter, the triggers that can launch a fear of driving are fairly clear. But the fears themselves can come in many flavours. Do any of these ring any bells with you? Note down any that do.

## Fear of learning to drive
Whilst we may have a picture in our minds of the carefree teenage driver who's raring to go, this isn't the situation for everybody, and some people find it hard to even get started driving.

Therapist Phil Parker, who has worked with thousands of clients worldwide, including Hollywood actors and rock stars, explains that fear of learning to drive is much more common than we might expect:

> 'It's very common for two main reasons. Firstly it's one of those coming of age moments which has so much significance for our future; so there's a fair amount of pressure – freedom from relying on parents to ferry us around; being able to impress others with our sophisticated skill set and so on.
>
> And secondly because it involves learning such an unfamiliar and different set of skills and actions than we are used to. The coordination of our feet for the biting point, combined with an awareness of what's going on in front, behind and beside us, along with a calculation of what the velocity is, and going to be, of the other potentially unpredictable road users.
>
> Additionally there are stringent exams; examiners who are, at least in our imaginations, fierce and unpleasant; and the more we fail to grasp the skills or to pass the test, and the longer we are bereft of the skill that everyone else seems to be able to master, the worse we feel about our abilities.'
> www.philparker.org

*Molly's story*
Molly Forbes overcame her fear of learning to drive to become confident behind the wheel. And although the fear resurfaced when she had a baby and took a break from driving, she's fought hard not to let it take over:

> 'It took me a while to "get the hang" of driving and, thankfully, I had a very patient and calm female instructor, which definitely helped.

I found the old fears of driving returned after I had my baby and I really had to force myself to get behind the wheel again. I think the fact I hadn't driven for a few weeks coupled with the huge responsibility of having my tiny baby in the car with me made me lose all confidence. I'm glad I forced myself to get on with it though, because now I'm very relaxed about driving. I hope it continues as I really don't want to pass any of my fears onto my daughter when she grows up.'

So Molly's initial anxiety, which could have developed into a much bigger phobia, was luckily nipped in the bud. Note that she had to force herself to keep driving to get more comfortable with it though – she didn't hang around waiting to feel more confident about it. She recognised that confidence grows when we push ourselves, so that's what she did.

## When stressful driving is your default setting

In recent years, studies have identified increasing cases of driving anxiety amongst armed forces personnel returning from overseas postings – these soldiers had been trained to drive with caution and avoid debris which might contain concealed bombs. You can see how this could turn into a heightened sense of anxiousness whilst driving when the soldier returns to civilian life – he's just not used to driving in a relaxed, stress-free way.

A report in the *New York Times* in January 2012 found an Army reservist, recently returned from combat duty 'avoiding cramped parking lots without obvious escape routes. She straddled the middle line, as if bombs might be buried in the curbs.'

So it's not surprising that someone like this who's been specially trained to drive in an unrelaxed way may have to re-learn their responses in order not to drive like there's a bomb under every road.

**Fear of motorways**

This is one of the most common types of fear of driving. Currently in the UK learner drivers are not allowed on to motorways, but the government has announced plans to change this, probably before the end of 2012, so that learner drivers get the chance to practice motorway driving with an instructor before they take their test.

Confident drivers say (and the research supports this) that a motorway is one of the safest places to drive. All the traffic is going in the same direction. There are no turns to navigate – simply drift off into a slip road when you want to exit.

When I was attempting to start driving again I always hated, hated, hated driving on motorways more than anything, and it was the last part of my phobia to go. As the speed of the car increased, so did the shakes in my hand. What I really disliked was the feeling of being trapped – no turning off into a side street when it all gets a bit much. You're there, trapped in the flow for the duration.

These days I try and look at it as a confident driver would – they're very straightforward roads to drive, so less worry about getting lost or taking a wrong turn. They get you where you're going, faster. You can usually see quite far ahead so less chance of nasty surprises. And feeling calm and confident on a motorway drive shows me that I've finally put this fear of driving in the past, where it belongs.

*Harry's story*

Though he's overcome his driving phobia, Harry still sticks to routes he knows:

> 'I hate motorways and busy A roads. It literally brings me out in a sweat if I think I might accidentally end up on one of these busy roads! It seems to be a fear of getting lost.'

I think Harry could do with investing in a Sat Nav. When your fear is focused on getting lost, this is one area where technology can be a huge help.

Bigger roads are one of the major sticking points for people who don't like driving. But here's the kicker: in fact, the statistics show that if you have to drive, doing it on the motorway is one of the safest places you can be. Figures from the UK government Department of Transport show that in 2010 most fatalities happened on rural and urban roads, with only 6% of fatalities taking place on motorways. And you can further tell that this is the case from the way these crashes are reported – a major motorway crash is big news. If it were an everyday occurrence then it simply wouldn't be reported in the same way – it would be a minor item on page 11 and probably not make the TV news at all.

However, as we know a phobia is not a rational thing. It does not respect statistics or bald facts. In 2011 a survey of almost 14,000 Automobile Association members, found that only 44% of women said they felt confident driving on the motorway.

But these are the facts, and are worth reminding yourself of. So if you have decided to avoid the motorways and take the back roads instead, effectively you are making the decision to travel on statistically less safe roads. Even if you don't believe it in your heart – use this information in your head if you have to travel on the motorway and you don't want to – repeat out loud if necessary: 'I'm safer here'.

And if you do come across those news reports of road accidents – avoid them as much as you can. Turn the page, click away from the website, switch off the news. It's not helping you to know about this stuff. You may find that you're drawn to those stories as much as they repel you, since they confirm your worst fears about driving. As we look, so shall we find, and if you're looking for a half empty glass then you're already on the way to finding one. But you will not help yourself by increasing the store of scary pictures in your imagination.

**Fear of being stationary in traffic**

If you're afraid of driving, you might assume that being stopped in traffic would be far less scary – after all, the cars aren't going anywhere, so far less potential to crash. But for some people, being in a car that's stopped is just as bad, if not worse, than being in one that's moving.

In particular, people with this fear don't like being stopped at road works or getting caught up in traffic jams. It's essentially a fear of being trapped and not being able to get out of the car if you want to – in that sense it's very similar to fear of motorways.

**Fear of parking**

A study in 2011 by Ford Motors into attitudes to parallel parking identified a high level of what's been dubbed 'Park-o-phobia'. The poll of 1,026 participants revealed:

- 12% of women drivers felt parallel parking was more stressful than a job interview and a visit to the dentist;
- Young drivers (16-24) and older drivers (55-64) rated parallel parking more stressful than a visit from the in-laws, Christmas shopping and motorway driving;
- 66% of men think they are better parallel parkers whereas 17% of women think they are better – overall, 55% of drivers think men are better whilst 10% think women are better;
- Only 3% of men rated women higher whereas 42% of women rated men higher;
- 50% of women admitted needed more than one attempt whilst only 29% of men admitted this;
- In general 39% of drivers needed more than one attempt.

Now, this survey was done to promote new technology fitted in some cars designed to help you park. So from that perspective it was designed to find that people had a problem with parking.

But really it makes sense that if driving makes you anxious, confident parking is unlikely to be top of your skill set either. Or is it just me who travels long distances to find a space three cars long to park in? Frankly, these days I am so relieved to be driving that parking is the least of it. It's a skill to master in time.

## People who drive even though they hate it

I was surprised to find that many of those who are scared of driving still have to do so out of necessity. So chew on this for a moment – at least some of those people that you see in cars and assume are confident drivers are just as scared as you.

Think about that next time you're out and about – look at other people in their cars and know that they share at least some of the feelings you have. Perhaps you're more confident than they are.

In some ways I think it's good that people like this are out there – they don't take driving for granted and are more likely to be cautious than carefree and taking chances. They are concentrating hard on driving safely, which is a lot better than if they weren't. And every day, they're battling their fears. They refuse to stay at home and be beaten and let their world be dictated to by fear. That's quite inspirational really, though I suspect these people don't feel like they're being particularly inspiring at all.

*Ken's story*

Ken says his fear of driving is terrible, even though he does it every day:

> 'I drive almost every day, but going anywhere new terrifies me. If anyone invites me out or I have to go anywhere new I think about it for a week beforehand. I like driving early in the morning or at night when the roads are quiet and it's easy to park. Very few friends know the true extent of my fears – it's like my dirty little secret.'

Again Ken has found a way to manage his fears – by sticking as much as possible to roads he knows or when there's not much traffic about. And even though he doesn't like new journeys, he still takes them – given enough notice. I wonder what difference it would make if he was more open about his attitude to driving? Might he get some feedback that he's a better driver than he thinks he is? Might he find that many other people feel the same, and gain comfort from that? I suspect so.

*Claire's story*
Claire is another driver who finds that her fear severely limits where she'll go:

> 'In the winter I may as well hibernate as I refuse point blank to drive anywhere. My child doesn't understand why when it's snowing I won't take the car to the school and instead make him walk. Poor little lad!
>
> If I'm comfortable with the road and know where I'm going and have got used to that road then great, I enjoy driving at this point. But today I went into a town and the roundabout had changed and there were so many lanes and new traffic lights I was like OMG OMG OMG and literally had my brother who can't drive guiding the wheel for me.'

It's interesting to note that even Claire, for whom fear of driving clearly is a big deal, still has little pockets of time where she enjoys driving. I think that with some help she could expand those pockets to include other parts of her driving life as well.

**Fear of bridges**
Even though this is essentially a combination of two phobias (heights and driving), a reluctance to drive over bridges is still fairly common.

*Ian's story*

Ian found that a fear of heights led to a more specific fear of driving over bridges:

'Driving over bridges was a real problem, because you need to remain in control for the safety of yourself and other drivers, and a phobia robs you of control. Of course, all you need to do is keep going straight, but that would be utterly terrifying. After a few years of this, it began to annoy the hell out of me.'

Ian's response is interesting in that instead of being a passive victim of his fear, he started to get angry with it – and this is what ultimately led to him tackling and overcoming it.

Do you ever get angry with your fear of driving? I don't mean angry with yourself for being fearful, but angry with the fear itself? Sometimes this can be a good way to start to see the fear not as an intrinsic part of yourself, but as something external which you can deal with and move away from.

## Fear of other drivers

Sometimes it's not you that's the problem – it's everyone else. Have you ever watched old home movie footage of roads in the 1960's and 70's? They look like fantastic places to drive – barely any cars at all, and those that are there are moving at a stately pace. (Hey, could that be another possible solution? Let's all find a time machine and pile in).

*Kate's story*

Kate Brian is a 48-year old writer who's more bothered by the other traffic than the act of driving.

'If I knew I could drive twenty miles without meeting another car, it wouldn't worry me nearly as much. The only time I've ever met a number of other people who didn't drive was when I did an MA in Creative Writing and there were a group of us who didn't drive at all which was really unusual. I sometimes wonder if it's something to do with having an overactive imagination. The moment I am behind the wheel of a car, I am imagining ghastly crashes whereas most people are thinking about getting to the shops.'

I think Kate's observation about the group of writers who didn't drive is interesting – some experts have put forward the theory that people with very active imaginations are more prone to developing phobias. So could it be that the thing that makes someone a creative person can also lead to problems? If you have a tendency towards an over-active imagination, keep reminding yourself of what's real and what's not.

**Range anxiety**

This term has been coined to refer to drivers of electric vehicles' fear of running out of power with nowhere to recharge. It refers to a fear that the car doesn't have enough range or power left in its battery and therefore may stop working during a journey, leaving the driver and passengers stranded.

It's a very specific, mechanical attitude rather than a more deep-seated phobia. If you are looking for help online for your driving anxiety then you may find yourself pulling up stories about how far an electric car can go. It may be a form of fear, but it's a long way from being a phobia. So if you have fear of driving, perhaps it's best to avoid electric cars, as it could potentially be one more thing to worry about.

If you do have an electric car, the best way to avoid range anxiety is by getting to know your vehicle as much as possible, particularly with regard to its battery capabilities, so that you are in no doubt as to how far it can go depending on the level of charge. A good navigation system will also help as you can clearly see how long your intended journey is and make a judgement based on that as to whether you have enough battery power to get you there, or whether you need to plan to stop and recharge.

### Fear of driving backwards

I think we need to take this one with a Hollywood A-lister sized pinch of salt.

In an interview with *Empire Magazine* in 2011, actor Brad Pitt claimed to have a driving-related phobia – he can't drive back to where he's just been. Pitt was quoted as saying: 'If I'm driving down the road and I miss a turn, I have to keep going forward. I can't reverse. It's some kind of psychological defect. I don't know the reason why... But it's just that, for better or worse, I want to keep moving on. I don't like to go backwards. It's not what I'm good at.'

I'm not sure that there are many lessons in that for us mere mortals, but at least if anyone ever questions your odd driving habits, at least you can say – 'Hey, if it's good enough for Brad Pitt...'.

### Driving as a cure for anxiety

With all these various types of road-related fears, you may be interested to know of the flip side – that some people use driving as a way to cope with anxiety. In particular, people with social anxiety (who feel anxious in social settings) sometimes prefer driving because it means they can be in a sealed world of their own that no one else can penetrate. It's a means to escape situations you find uncomfortable, and be in more control of where you're going and how. It doesn't work for everyone, since some people with SA still find being around other drivers too challenging, or can only drive by themselves, but for those who enjoy it, driving can be a wonderful escape.

So from that perspective, for some people, driving is a solution rather than a problem. You choose when you arrive and leave. You're in total control of your environment – the temperature, the ambience, the destination. You choose what music's playing, and whether or not you want to talk, sing or swear. No strangers are coming in unless you ask them. You can simply enjoy the rhythm of the miles disappearing under your wheels and feel good about it. When you look at it from that angle, driving in your car could be a pretty pleasant place to be.

## Success story
*Ian's story revisited: overcoming fear of bridges*
Ian, whom we met a few pages ago, has now managed to overcome the fear of driving over bridges which developed in his twenties:

> 'I developed a few tricks that helped. I would mentally recite the alphabet backwards when crossing bridges. This seemed to tie up enough of my mind to make the phobia less powerful. I also decided that, if I was unable to stop my reaction to bridges, I could at least rewrite what that reaction was. I began telling myself that the feeling I got when on bridges was excitement, and that I should look forward to crossing them because I found it such a thrill. This was surprisingly successful.
>
> In the end, however, I turned 40 and thought "I'm 40 now, I can't be bothered being scared of anything anymore" and for some reason that worked. I'll cross any bridge that you like now.'

# 3. Why drive? What's so great about driving anyway?

Often the fear that driving phobics feel is vastly out of proportion with the reality of the situation. We fear things that haven't happened and aren't going to, and in doing so ignore the potential good things that are much more likely to happen. This chapter looks at the benefits of driving, and also what difference conquering this fear will make to your life.

We're starting to look at the good side of driving, and what becoming a confident driver has the potential to give us. Now we are taking our journey away from the fear, and towards somewhere better. Once you have a sense of where you want to go, it becomes a lot easier to get there.

Aside from the driving itself, we're looking at why it's important to deal with all of this and face up to your fears. And we look at the experience of people who make an active choice not to drive – could this be for you?

Essentially, what we're doing here is separating out the fear from the drive. I want to focus on the good stuff about driving, so you can see what difference it will make to your life to put this fear behind you once and for all. You have to want to do it to be able to do it, and for many people the underlying issue is that they simply don't really want to drive.

So what would it take for you to want to drive? What would it take to make it a fun and relaxing thing to do? What's so great about driving anyway? What are you losing by not driving? Take some time to write down the answers to those questions in your notebook.

*Helen's story*
Helen worries that her fear of driving is causing her life to stagnate:

'I would love to be able to drive though, being able to go places, visit my disabled friend who lives in the sticks. I would love to be able to apply for jobs that sound more suitable to me. Two years ago I had refresher driving lessons. The instructor didn't instill too much confidence in me and what was frustrating was that we never drove very far and to places I would go to, like the supermarket.'

Helen's story illustrates how important it is that if you do have refresher lessons you need to take charge and get them to suit you, to help you drive to the places you want to go to. Think about the driving you want to do, the journeys that would benefit your life, and base your lessons around those.

### Does it really matter if you don't drive?

We're always being told that taking the car is the less green option. In these days when we have to be careful of the planet's resources, plus take care of our own health, there are lots of times when it makes more sense to leave the car at home and walk instead.

And if you really wanted to spin it, you could convince yourself that opting out of the driving population is an active, safer lifestyle choice: No, it's not that I can't drive, it's more that I'm making a greener lifestyle choice. Yeah, right. You can fool everybody apart from yourself.

Now, contrary to appearances, I'm not here to simply wave a flag for driving and cars. When it gets down to it, I prefer walking too. All you have to do is head off out the door, breathe in the fresh air and go where your legs will take you. I love walking and always choose to do it for short local journeys, much to the annoyance of my children who'd rather have a ride in a nice warm car.

The big difference between driving and other types of phobias is that – if you choose to – you can avoid the experience fairly well. It's virtually impossible to avoid a spider, but if you choose to define yourself as a non driver, well, that's up to you. And if you live in a major city with good public transport links, or can afford to get taxis, then your problem may be solved already.

This is why some people, simply, choose not to drive at all. However, if this is a defensive decision as a result of a fear that's not been dealt with, what can happen is that the fear simply grows. So you can quite easily go from being an anxious driver to being an anxious passenger. And since it's virtually impossible to get through your life without getting in to a car at some point, this is why, even if you choose not to drive, you still need to deal with what's at the root of your fear.

*Jo's story*
Jo is aged 45, has never learnt to drive and doesn't intend to:

> 'Sometimes I think if only I could drive then the kids and I could be at the beach in 45 minutes – but then the train is only a bit longer.'

*Mary's story:*
Mary finds that her reluctance to drive affects her family life and the activities she does with her children. Unlike Jo, she finds that public transport is no consolation:

> 'I only sign the children up for activities that I can reach by train and we have to allow extra time. I think it's a bit pathetic for a 40 year old woman to be so silly about something that even Noddy can do and I'd love to be able to pull myself together.'

There is an enormous difference between making an active choice in your life to be a non-driver for environmental reasons, cost, or simply out of choice, and feeling that you have to be like that because you have been backed in to a corner by fear. The first is an act of choice – the second is a reaction to fear. And fear does not go away simply because you choose not to deal with it.

We have seen that fear of driving grows out of a combination of experience and life history, combined with stress. So if you are living with a fear that dictates the action you take in life, then you are living with stress. And that's the crusher. It's not about the car. It's about the effect the fear has on your mental wellbeing. And improving your mental wellbeing is the crucial part.

## Driving for fun?

Confident drivers who have never felt the fear of travel by road, take a very different view. In fact, some see driving as a method of relaxation in itself, as they take off for an aimless drive, simply to feel the miles roll away beneath them.

Or they see it as a means to an end, a way of getting from A to B, with no other feelings or emotional attachments. Or they might see it as thrilling and exciting, with the open road as a good place to be.

So if we take a lesson from confident drivers and aim to turn it into something that works for us, there's a lot that can be great about driving.

Elements of driving you can learn to love:
- The freedom to go anywhere you want;
- Not being reliant on others to take you places;
- Makes life a bit easier for whoever drives you now;
- Increased choices about where to work, visit and holiday;
- A space of your own that you can design just how you like it;
- You get to choose the music and ambience;
- Seeing friends who live far away;
- It shows that you are in control and have moved away from your fear.

*Take a confident drive and enjoy it*

Here's a little exercise to stretch your comfort zone. Drive to a place you like and are excited about going to (with a driving instructor if you need to), as a way of re-associating your driving with good feelings. Drive to a place that spells independence to you – a place you would like to go to. If you're not ready to drive yourself, ask someone else to do it. Focus on the destination rather than the journey.

And if you're not ready to do this at all – that's fine too. Instead, spend some time thinking about the places you intend to go to, and the fun that driving could bring you. Because one day it will. Don't beat yourself up about the things you're not doing because you're not driving – instead, assume that one day you will do those things, and make plans on that basis. Instead of thinking 'I wish I wasn't missing out on X', turn that thought to 'I'm looking forward to the day I do X'. Make it an open, future possibility rather than a closed regret.

### Be the driver you wish everyone else was

As we noted in Chapter One, for many people it is the experience of a crash that will have triggered their fear of driving in the first place. And though you only have a very small chance of being involved in a further crash, this can be a hard one to get past if you're to regain your driving confidence. But think of it this way – you are not protected from crashing by not driving, as you could still be involved in a crash as a passenger. Yes I know that's not particularly cheery but at least it's honest.

However, as the driver you are far more in control of the situation as you can choose to drive as safely as possible. So you don't drive when you're sleepy or have had a drink, you don't drive too close to the car in front and you keep to the speed limit etc. You'll drive courteously and let people out at turnings. Choose to be the sort of driver that you wish everyone else was. At least that way, there's one more of you on the road.

*Babar's story*
Babar Coughlan is a 46-year old mother of two boys. She feels that it's the aggressiveness of other drivers that puts her off:

'I would have preferred driving back in the 60's when people were not "rush, rush RUSH" and JUST WAITING to jump down your throat if you get something wrong – probably a sign of our times.'

But if we let these other drivers, plus our fear, beat us, what do we stand to miss out on? Many things.

*Lucy's story*
Lucy found that the effects of not driving rippled through her whole life and made it harder in many ways:

'We lived in London and were doing up our first flat. There was a DIY superstore about half an hour's walk from our house (but only 5 minutes' drive). I preferred to walk there and back carrying bricks and compost and cement powder than drive, which was, of course, bloody hard work and took ages. It affected my social life and also my confidence in general. I felt utterly stupid and ridiculous and it was something other people found very hard to understand.'

I think many of us will be nodding in agreement with this kind of situation – the ridiculous knots that we tie ourselves up into when a simple drive would have been so much easier. Driving phobia robs you of that choice and makes every journey a potential source of stress.

*Deborah's story*
Writer Deborah Riccio finds that her fear of driving has hurt her life in many ways, though she forces herself to do it:

'The biggest "thing" I missed out on was a get-together in Manchester of all the on-line writing friends I've made over the past eight years or so. The event was a book launch of my best writing buddy. I knew I wouldn't be able to relax and enjoy myself. I knew that even if I got there, I'd be worried about having to get in a taxi from/to the event, scared to get in somebody else's car, nervous about the amount of traffic in a big city like Manchester. I felt a total wet blanket when I said I wouldn't be going.'

Deborah's fear is so severe that it's developed from fear of driving and into fear of being driven and being in heavy traffic. And this has in turn clamped down on her social life and led to her missing out on wonderful, important events like this. This thing snakes its tendrils everywhere. You can see why tackling it is so vital.

## My mother, my role model
As we noted in Chapter One, having a parent who's reluctant to drive is one of the contributing factors in developing this fear. So the effects on family life go far beyond a reluctance to sign your child up for football lessons on the other side of town. You could be planting the seeds for a future fear. You could be the role model that stops your child becoming a confident driver. Or you could be a role model for addressing and overcoming your fears—which do you want to be?

## Getting back in control
Why does a simple thing like driving have the power to turn a mild mannered individual into a screaming monster, and a normally composed person into a gibbering wreck? It's all about control, or lack of it.

A phobia is generally a fear without a justifiable reason, where the fear is completely out of proportion with the genuine danger at hand. But this is where driving phobia is trickier than other phobias, because sufferers can genuinely convince themselves that driving is dangerous. And as we have seen, in many cases this feeling is borne out of a real experience if it happened as a result of a road traffic accident. This in turn serves as evidence that driving is, in fact, dangerous.

But driving can also be fun. It can bring you freedom and opportunities. It can support your life, rather than fear dragging you down. It helps to get you moving, rather than stagnating. Ultimately what we're seeking is a life we dictate, rather than one that's dictated to by fear.

## Success story
*Andrew's story: concentration and refresher lessons*
Andrew is a former police officer who found that refresher lessons helped restore his driving confidence.

'When I was a police officer, high-speed driving was part of the job and it never troubled me particularly – in fact I really loved it. In 2005 I had a crash going to a burglary in the early hours of the morning. I rolled the car and knocked myself out and although I had no lasting injuries it left me terrified of driving again. I was constantly convinced I was going to lose control, and literally every time I approached a corner I'd brace myself and expect to leave the road. Eventually I went for a refresher advanced driving course and got most of my confidence back.

Five years on from my crash my confidence has returned, although I'm a lot more cautious than I used to be, which is probably no bad thing.'

# 4. Stress relief: how to deal with driving-related stress

So before we go anywhere near the car, we're going to spend some time sorting out our minds and bodies so we'll be in better shape when we get there. In this chapter we're looking into one of the main factors in fear of driving – stress. As we already discovered, stress is a very big part of the reason why some people and not others develop driving phobia.

Many of the contributing factors for this condition are historical events that you can't do anything about – you can't change the fact that your parent may not have been a confident driver, or the fact that you were involved in some sort of car crash, or had a life changing event happen.

But the contributing factor that pushes these into something approaching a phobia is stress and anxiety – and that is something you can work on. So it makes sense to start by looking at the parts of the picture you can change, rather than those you can't.

Here we are looking at practical ways you can deal with stress and feel calmer before you start driving. Many of these suggestions are things you can do at home without getting into a car. This includes advice from practitioners in the field with suggestions for things you can do directly before you drive. Some may appeal to you more than others – there's no 'one size fits all' solution to stress, so keep your notebook at hand and write down anything that strikes you as something you could easily do to feel calmer. After that, make a note of WHEN you intend to do this – setting a definite date is crucial, because it takes the intended action away from 'something I might do, when I get round to it' and into 'something I intend to do'. It turns a vague idea into a definite goal.

And then if you can, tell someone close to you what you intend to do, and when you intend to do it. Bringing someone else into the equation makes it far, far more likely to happen, as you then have someone to call you on it if you don't do what you say you're going to. If you don't feel you have anyone in your life you can speak to about this, you can hire a professional life coach to help you out with this. When I'm coaching clients we always set some sort of action point as homework at the end of the session. Nobody wants to come back to the next session and admit that they didn't bother to do their homework, otherwise they would just be wasting their time and money on the sessions. Adding in that extra level of accountability makes a huge difference between the things we intend to do, but don't, and the goals that we actually follow through on.

Alternatively, you can also use an online support group to help you track your goals, but you will have to be much more committed and self-disciplined for this since there is less accountability and it's easier to drop out of groups like that.


**Less stress doesn't mean no stress**
When you're reading this chapter, I think it's important to bear in mind that you may not always be able to completely calm yourself before you step into the car, or when you're driving. Whilst there's a lot you can do to prepare yourself, sometimes even that may not be enough.

This particularly applies if the journey is one that you haven't chosen to make (and therefore feel less in control of before you start). Sometimes you may need to – in the words of Susan Jeffers' classic self help book – *Feel The Fear And Do It Anyway*. Because if you were planning to wait until you felt completely unstressed before you got in a car, you might find that that day never comes.

But the good news is that if you can get over the initial panic and nerves, you may find that they subside and that it isn't as bad as you feared. In fact it may be better. However you feel, don't use your lack of calm as yet another excuse not to drive. Telling yourself 'I'll drive when I don't feel so stressed' may simply be another avoidance tactic to put off conquering your fear. Life for all of us has its share of stresses and strains. There may never be a time when you reach a state of absolute equilibrium and calm. Sometimes you will need to drive, regardless of how you feel.

And also, if you have a go, you may find that your own inner reserves develop, so that you trust yourself to deal with any stress that arises.

**Expert tip: a little stress is good for you**
Tracy Dempsey is a coach who says that a small amount of stress can help rather than hinder you.

'A bit of stress is actually important for giving a good performance, so your goal isn't to completely relax, but to get into a state of calm focus.

Create a positive expectation of your performance; if you expect to do badly, you'll be more likely to make mistakes. Instead, visualise yourself driving well, performing manoeuvres easily and enjoying the drive. Pay attention to the words and phrases that come to mind when you think about driving; if you have recurring negative or anxious thoughts like "I hate parallel parking, I always mess it up", that will hold you back – change it to "I'm getting better at parallel parking, if I take it slowly, I can do it". (It has to be believable, so don't aim to move straight from "I hate this manoeuvre" to "I love it!") Worrying about unexpected problems can be very stressful, so take a phrase like "whatever happens, I'll handle it" as your mantra.

Practice confident body language; the way you sit and stand can affect your mood, so keep your head up, shoulders relaxed and smile when you want to feel calm and confident. The more often you practice these techniques,

the calmer and more in control you'll feel in any potentially stressful situation, not just driving.'
www.soulambition.co.uk

## What is stress for you?

Stress is a very widely used term used to indicate something
which has a negative impact on a person's physical and mental
wellbeing – literally, it's something that gets you down. But what
that something might be varies from person to person – one
person's stress inducer is another person's idea of fun. It might
not even be anything big; it could be the combination of lots of
little things over an extended period of time. As has been noted
earlier, it's the combination of already being highly stressed,
coupled with some sort of car-related incident, that most often
triggers driving phobia.

Even if you have not been aware of it before, think about
that for a few moments now – what do you see as the source of
your stress? What was happening in your life during the time
leading up to you becoming fearful of driving? It could be a
major life change such as having a new baby, new job or getting
divorced. Whatever it is, look for it and acknowledge it now.
Have you really dealt with it as well as you could? Are there parts
of it that you're still angry or upset about? What can you do to
resolve this? What will you do? What do you need to let go of?
Write down the answers to these questions in your notebook.

If you are not currently driving and don't need to in the immediate future then you may find it more helpful to put it aside
completely for now. Give yourself permission to not even try to
drive, and instead spend some time working on your stress levels
and mental health generally.

Keep a moods diary for a month or so and note the link between how you feel and what else is going on in your life, and
particularly how anxious or stressed you feel.

**Look for your natural de-stressors**

Just as the cause of stress is different for every person, there's no 'one size fits all' approach to becoming more relaxed and less stressed either. I find exercising very relaxing, whilst some people find that even thinking about the gym brings them out in hives.

Think about the things that work for you to keep you relaxed and aim to do them every day, regardless of how stressed you feel that day. It's almost like taking a vitamin pill or preventative medicine to keep your reserve levels high. Don't wait until you feel more stressed – one thing you can assume from the fact that you are currently experiencing fear of driving is that your stress levels are or have been higher than your mind can cope with. Anything you can do to address this will help. So think about:

- What are the areas of your life that drain you, and what can you do about that?
- What are the things in life that energise and relax you – and how can you do more of them?

Make these lists in your notebook now.

**Do something physical**

Anything which makes you concentrate on your physical body rather than all the thoughts whizzing round in your head will act as a natural de-stressor. And you don't have to be at all sporty to do this – it's about losing yourself in an activity; engaging, rather than exerting yourself, physically. And don't be afraid to get your hands dirty. This could mean:

- Going for a run;
- Playing with children – modeling with Play Doh, making sandcastles or building games such as Lego;
- Taking an exercise class. Even better if it's something fairly vigorous where you can sweat out your frustrations;
- Walking (not the sort of walking you do when you're avoiding driving, but choosing to walk somewhere you enjoy);

- Yoga;
- Gardening;
- Baking cakes or kneading bread;
- Painting or drawing;
- Decorating pottery;
- Doing a challenging jigsaw;
- Household repairs, such as putting up shelves or scraping wallpaper off a wall;
- Spending time with animals – groom that pony, walk that dog, stare at a goldfish or cuddle a cat. Animals are great de-stressors because they don't judge you and they don't know your history or what else is going on in your life. They simply respond to how you are in the here and now, and are usually happy to see you (especially if you've got food for them).

Which of these can you do, starting this week? Or perhaps there's something else physical that you'd enjoy doing? Write down any ideas that appeal to you in your diary now, setting a date for when you intend to do them.

### Meditation

Meditation can be great for helping to clear your head, but for people with an already anxious mind that's whirring with thoughts, it's a big challenge to get your mind to a point where it can be still.

For this reason, you may find a guided meditation a useful place to start, as then you have someone else's voice to concentrate on. This can be done either in a meditation class or via a meditation CD or download. There are many of these commercially available, either at low cost or free, so pick one depending on whether you think you'll respond to a male or female voice and if you have any preference over regional accents. I like the American spiritual teacher Dr Wayne Dyer, who has a lovely deep, calming voice. See the resources section at the back of this book for specific recommendations.

The other advantage of listening to a guided meditation is that you can do it very easily from home by downloading a recording. You will need space and time to do it, but it's not difficult to carve this out if you want to – either get up or go to bed slightly earlier than usual. You could listen to one as you're drifting off to sleep. Many of these recordings are around the 20 minute mark so even if you've never tried meditation before, have an open mind and give it 20 minutes of your time.

## Aromatherapy

Aromatic plants and oils have been used for thousands of years for medical and other purposes. The good thing about using aromatherapy and the calming power of scent is that you can very easily carry it over in to your driving. Even if you're new to aromatherapy, think about how your car smells, how you react to that, and whether you want it to smell differently – it's all part of taking control of that environment and turning it into a place you want to be.

Liz Williams is a Complementary Therapist specialising in holistic treatment including aromatherapy. Liz says that aromatherapy can help with the emotions of fear and the stress and anxiety of driving by choosing suitable essential oils:

'These may include: orange, bergamot, marjoram, geranium, rose, sandalwood, neroli and ylang ylang.

A pleasant way to keep the aroma would be to use a couple of drops on a handkerchief or on a cotton wool ball and keep it in the car during the drive. If the oils are to be used in a massage, always use a trained aromatherapist as it is very important not to use too much as this can have adverse effects on the body. If citrus oils are used during a massage, activities in the sun or on a sun bed should be avoided. Regular aromatherapy massages will also help to reduce stress and release tension and fear. An example of oils selected to help with stress

- Basil;
- Marjoram;
- Sandalwood;
- Bergamot;
- Geranium;
- Neroli.

When buying an essential oil, always choose oils that are stated as 100% essential oil that is trusted from a reputable supplier. Some oils can be "adulterated" and altered for cheaper, or synthetic oils and this will affect the quality and therapeutic value of the original oil. If in doubt, speak to a trained aromatherapist.'
www.orchid-therapies.co.uk


## Visualisation

Creative visualisation is a technique that's been around for over 100 years and is used by many therapists to apply to many different situations. It's also commonly used by athletes to improve their performance. In essence, it's a focused, detailed, repeated daydream. As adults we probably don't daydream enough, or if we do, we focus on the bad stuff and call it worrying. But positive daydreaming is a very effective way to reduce your levels of stress and convince your mind that you can do what you intend to.

You can start creative visualisation by simply imagining that you're doing something successfully, even if you haven't done it yet. Do this enough times and when you come to do whatever you've been visualising, your brain is effectively fooled into thinking 'Oh yes, I can do this, I've been here before and all went well.' Golfers use this technique to imagine hitting the perfect stroke, so that eventually their mind believes they can do it and thinks that they've done it before.

So, for example, as a coach if I'm working with someone who's nervous about a job interview I will encourage them to visualise walking into the interview room, feeling confident, answering questions with ease and shaking hands with their interviewers because everything's gone well. You might want to try this technique if you have a driving test coming up – imagine yourself walking away from the test site feeling happy, and your examiner congratulating you for having passed your driving test.

So let's apply the creative visualisation technique to driving. Now, the obvious thing to do would be to spend some time visualising yourself as a happy, calm and confident driver, enjoying your journey. And if you can do that, then brilliant. Keep doing that and those driving daydreams will help you with your real life drives.

But for some people, even this is a step too far – as soon as they start to think about themselves driving, the fear becomes overwhelming and pushes out the more positive thoughts. So if you find this happens, a good workaround is to take the car out of the equation and instead visualise yourself having driven somewhere successfully. Who would you visit? What would you like to see? Who would your ultimate driving companion be? Maybe a movie star or someone you admire? Where would you go?

It's important with visualisations to do them repeatedly, so it really gets embedded in to your subconscious mind.

- Sit or lie down somewhere comfortable, close your eyes and take your mind there. Either imagine a route you plan to take, or make one up;
- Take at least 10 minutes to focus on your daydream;
- Take your time and repeat it as often as possible, every day if you can, and not less than twice a week;
- Each time you repeat the exercise, add more detail and colour to the picture until it feels more and more real;
- If you start to feel panicky because you're thinking about driving, stick with it until the feeling passes.

I still do this sort of visualisation regularly when I have a new drive coming up that I'm slightly nervous about. I imagine myself at the end of the drive, getting out of the car in a good mood, feeling pleased that I've got to my destination. Sometimes I look up images of my destination on Google Earth, to make it easier to imagine being there. So essentially, I'm giving my mind the assumption that I will do this drive successfully, and I will enjoy doing it.

Visualisation is a great help for confident driving, since instead of worrying about what might happen when you drive, you're taking control and assuming that it will all go well.

**Expert tip: recall your past successes**
Chartered Psychologist Dr Rick Norris has this tip for improving your driving confidence:

> 'I would advise that people start to increase their confidence by recalling all the car journeys they have successfully undertaken. A particularly challenging journey that was successful would make a very good example of something they could visualise before they set off.
>
> Replaying the memory of a successful past event in real detail often increases people's belief that they can replicate the success. They could do this whilst sitting in the car before they start the engine. Closing your eyes and replaying the memory using all your senses and paying particular attention to how great you felt when you were successful is the essence of this technique.'

**Eliminate the negative**
Of course, as well as taking on new practices, the other way to approach the sources of stress in your life is to see how you can cut them out, or at least learn to handle them better.

This may not always be practical – if your source of stress was becoming a parent, it's not as if you can send the baby back. But you can start to ask yourself – what do I need to do differently to help this become an enjoyable experience?

And if the source of your stress is something you can change, it may be a big shift, but if it's affecting your life to this degree then it probably will have to change eventually. How long do you intend on doing that job that you hate, or putting up with people who stress you out, or living in a place you don't want to come home to? Your driving phobia could be a wakeup call for some major life changes that need to be made.

Take a few moments to think about that now and write down any longer term goals that spring to mind. What do you want to have changed in your life in ten years' time? Once you've written down that goal, from there you can work back along the time line and then write down where you want to be in five years' time? How about in a year? Six months? Work back from the long term goal to help you see what action you need to take in your immediate future.

**Expert tip: watch comedies before you drive**
Hypnotherapist Dominic Knight says that we need to address the messages we give ourselves:

> '95% of what we feel is based on how we are communicating with ourselves. When a person has a fear of driving they keep focusing on the previous discomforts and they are not focusing on how well they used to drive. The key is to change how you represent it to yourself and feel really good.'

And if visualisation is not for you, Dominic has a much more fun suggestion:

'Watch comedies and at the point of laughter think about driving well. What this does is create a new response in the brain and helps collapse the previous trigger of fear. Also ensure before driving you feel totally relaxed and visualize driving comfortably. The subconscious part of the mind cannot differentiate between something real and something imagined hence if you keep imagining driving well, you would experience that in your reality.'

## The de-stressing potential of music

We'll look at this in more detail in the chapter on panic attacks, but music can help with any levels of stress – as long as it's the right music. Music connects with us in a physical and emotional way, and different types of music will affect you in different ways. Now I must admit that it was a long time before I could bear to have any sort of music playing in the car, but when I did – oh, what a difference.

Best of all is if you can play a track you really love that will lift you up and have you singing along, naturally drawing your focus away from your fear.

Why not make a special mix CD of songs you really love, to listen to when you're driving? These could be songs that connect with a time in your life when you felt better than you do now, less stressed and more confident.

And even if you're not driving at all right now – still make that CD. It's a signal to your subconscious that one day you will be out there driving again and singing along with pride.

Alternatively, if you're not a big music fan you can listen to audio books, a language course or comedy recording when driving – anything to engage your brain in a different way and distract you from focusing on the fear. This will make it easier for you to concentrate on driving in a calmer way. As mentioned above, you may not be able to do this straight away, as you may start off feeling that you need to concentrate 100% on driving and driving alone. But you will eventually pass through this stage, and that's where audio can help. Think of it like an advanced stage of moving towards being a confident driver.

The great thing about designing your own driving music is that you are taking ownership of your driving conditions and turning your car into a fun place to be. And whilst it might seem right now that fun is the last thing on your mind when it comes to driving, it's crucial that you start to see it in a more positive light. It can be a world that you're in charge of.

## Adopt a positive mantra

Hypnotherapist Barbara Ford-Hammond advises developing your own personal mantra to say out loud either before or during driving. This could be: 'I am in control'. 'I am safe'. 'I love to drive'. 'I enjoy my independence' repeated. Whatever you say, it should be positive and in the present tense, affirming that this is how you are now (or how you want to be).

I most commonly say 'I am a calm and confident driver', which then contracts to 'Calm and confident, calm and confident' repeated over and over again if I start to get a bit panicky, and 'Calm, calm, calm' if I am really starting to freak out. I may not feel particularly calm or confident at the time, but the point of doing this is to take your focus into a better place and give your mind something more positive to aim at. And it does work. Eventually your mind gets so bored of you going on about this calm stuff that it decides that it might as well go there, if only to shut you up. At least that's my theory.

A very useful thing to do can be to write out your positive mantra on a post-it note and stick it where you can't help but see it regularly – on your computer screen for example, or on your bathroom mirror. Only do this if everyone else in your house is the understanding type and not liable to make fun of your mantra. There's a reason why 'Keep Calm and Carry On' is a popular poster – it's become a bit of a cliché, but at heart it's a good saying to adopt. We all have times in life when we need to keep calm and carry on – literally, if we're driving.

## Expert opinion: pre-driving breathing and relaxation exercises

Barbara Ford Hammond recommends:

'Three breaths and on each breath out say to yourself (1) I am calm (2) I am focused (3) I have control. Breathe out fully or tension remains lurking and hurting.

Identify where in your body the tension is and imagining breathing or mentally massaging it away.

If your tummy is a mass of butterflies imagine them as a favourite colour and have them fly in formation.

Think of the area around the navel as a diamond-shape of muscle and breathe fully in and out of the there. It can help to put your hands in the shape using thumbs and forefingers (I use this with anyone that has performance anxiety).

Create an anchor or trigger for calm/control by imagining feeling good and then touching ear or thigh or doing an action like squeezing thumb and finger together.'

Anxiety expert Charles Linden says that simple breathing and visualisation exercises can be an effective way to prime yourself prior to any stressful event.

'Stand with your legs shoulder width apart and then raise your arms from your side to shoulder level slowly to the count of five and then down slowly to the count of five allowing your hands to cross in front of you at waist height and then smoothly repeat. Do this for one minute. You can do this as often as you like with your eyes open or closed; it can be a useful device when practised regularly.'

**Expert tip: peripheral vision relaxation technique**
Therapist Phil Parker is a leading personal development expert with a background in NLP and hypnosis. This is his advice:

'The best solution for leaving your fear of driving behind is to get some targeted help. All that's happened is that you have developed a strong "nervousness" response to the whole idea of driving. It could happen to anyone, it doesn't mean you're weak, stupid or incapable, it just means you need to relearn how to feel confident about driving and about your abilities. And that's surprisingly easy to achieve as long as you have the right help. Trying to break through the fear by sticking with the lessons is sometimes all you need, but if the fear is already well established it is likely to just get compounded and worsen your confidence.

For general calming down I'd recommend the peripheral vision relaxation technique, which works like this:
- Focus on a spot about 45 degrees above your eye line – keep your head level and look up at the spot with your eyes;
- Whilst still focusing on that spot in front of you, slowly start to notice the objects in your peripheral vision, without directly looking at them – an easy way to do this is to touch your ears and then move your hands out to the side, noticing as they start to appear in your view.

Doing this has the effect of changing your brain waves to the more relaxing alpha and theta waves. The more you practice the easier it is to get in to this relaxing state where pressures seem less important and you find you can refocus on being calm and confident for the upcoming driving lesson or test.'

Phil's also a fan of positive language and images to help you keep calm:

'If you have any negative internal voices, for example a voice that says "You will never be able to do this well" then use this relaxation exercise to rise above those voices and chose to say some positive things to replace them in your mind.

It's vital that you form these new thoughts properly; watch out for "negative wants" such as "I want to not be really scared" – a good way of explaining why this is a problem is to notice what you think of when you try not to think of the Queen juggling 12 purple monkeys! So if you use the thought "I want to not be really scared" it will unfortunately just prepare your body to be really scared. Instead say it positively and use an image "I want to be as calm as a puppy dozing in the sun".'

### Expert advice: pre-driving relaxation exercises

These pre-driving relaxation exercises are from therapist Phil Parker:

'This is a great exercise to do before you go anywhere near a car:
- A few hours before the driving lesson use the peripheral vision relaxation technique [as described previously] to get nice and relaxed;
- Then in your mind, whilst feeling those relaxed feelings, imagining putting your hands in the 10 to 2 position on the steering wheel. This connects the relaxing feelings with feelings of holding the steering wheel;
- Repeat until the thought of touching the steering wheel brings on feelings of calmness;
- Repeat steps 1-3 replacing the steering wheel with images of other elements of the car driving experience. The feeling of the seatbelt across you, the feel

of the gear stick lever, the pedal under your feet and so on.

Above all, remember why you're doing this. In your mind make sure you're recognising how important and worthwhile it is going to be for you, how great you'll feel when you are a confident experienced driver, and remind yourself – if all those other people can do it, then of course you can too!'

## Importance of diet: watch what you eat and drink

What we put into our bodies and how our bodies then feel are of course inextricably linked. You'll find more information on this in the chapter on panic attacks.

Obviously it goes without saying that you should not be having any kind of alcohol before you drive. Yes I know that there are legal limits and those limits are not zero, but if you are prone to stress around driving then just assume that they are.

The two main things to watch out for with regard to your stress levels are your blood sugar levels and levels of caffeine. Many people find that too much caffeine can increase anxiety levels, so cut back on the cola drinks and lay off the triple espressos.

Make sure you eat well and regularly in order to keep your blood sugar levels steady and stop you feeling faint when you least need to. Don't drive on an empty stomach. This is where you really need to listen to your body and think carefully about which foods support you and help you feel calm. Is there anything that needs to change about your daily eating habits? Does the stress you feel show up in what you eat, i.e. chaotic eating patterns, turning to food for comfort etc?

## Expert opinion: nutrition and anxiety

Registered nutritionist Dr Carina Norris says that although it would be too big a claim to say that food can cure anxiety, what you eat and drink certainly affects your energy levels and mood, with knock-on effects for your stress and anxiety levels.

'Your blood sugar plays a large part in governing your energy levels, and to a certain extent your mood. For example, if you go for too long without eating, your blood sugar level will fall, which can make you feel weak, jittery and even anxious.

For sustained energy and stable moods, what you need are stable blood sugar levels. Unless you suffer from diabetes, or impaired blood glucose control (which can lead to diabetes), your body is able to maintain its own blood sugar within safe levels. But some people are particularly sensitive to fluctuations in blood sugar, and can "feel" the weakness when they are getting low, and conversely may become "buzzy" when their blood sugar rises rapidly. And this roller-coastering feeling can lead to mood swings.

You can help keep your blood sugar – and your mood – stable by eating low glycaemic index (GI) foods, which provide slow-release energy, drip-feeding glucose into your bloodstream. Good examples of healthy low GI foods are wholegrains (such as wholemeal bread, brown rice, brown pasta, and oatmeal), nuts and seeds, lean meat, fish, eggs, low-fat dairy products, and fruit and vegetables.

On the other hand, high GI foods will cause a rapid spike in your blood sugar, but the energy it provides won't last, and your energy levels (and often your mood) will rapidly fall. The high GI foods are generally the sugary or highly refined ones – sugar, sweets, sugary fizzy drinks, biscuits and the like. And products made from white flour have a higher GI than those made from wholemeal. Fruit juice also has a high GI – the natural sugars have been "released", so they can hit your blood-

stream faster than if you'd had to eat, and digest, the whole fruit.'
www.carinanorris.co.uk


## Medication to help you deal with anxiety and stress

I don't want to give specific names of drugs here, since the medication that's available changes all the time and is something you need to discuss in confidence with your own doctor.

If your anxiety is very severe, and you have tried some of the tips described in this chapter but have not felt an improvement, talk to your doctor. Don't go looking on the internet; you need to talk to a professional who knows your medical history for this. Your doctor will ascertain whether medication might help and prescribe whatever they see as necessary – if your doctor feels that you show signs of depression, or if you are already taking other medication, then this will affect what's prescribed.

Even with this, there is no such thing as a magic pill, so give the medication a few weeks to work – some work more quickly than others, depending on what they are. But luckily, we are now in an era where people take medication for all kinds of reasons. Mental health is an issue just as physical health is. And if you need professional help for your health, go get it. Anything's better than continuing to suffer.

And when you're at it, keep going with other forms of anxiety and stress relief, so that eventually you'll be able to cope with these feelings by yourself and without the help of medication. Pills can be a fantastic help for some people, but they're not a forever solution and they're not for everybody.

Aim to walk away from your stress on your own two feet (or your own four wheels) – but accept that we all need a little support sometimes.

**How to build your driving confidence: the pot plant theory**
People who've come to me for life coaching because they want to increase their confidence will be familiar with the pot plant speech. No, not that type of pot plant. The pot plant speech is my theory of confidence.

I believe that many people who say they lack confidence treat it as if it were some kind of indoor plant. They hope that if they nurture it, it'll grow, and maybe one day they'll tuck it under their arm and take it out for a walk. So they say things like 'If I had more confidence I would quit my job/write a book/go driving/insert scary action of choice'.

But confidence doesn't work like that. It will not grow independently before you do things. It grows whilst you do them. So if you're waiting until you feel more confident until you get back in the car, then you probably need to just go ahead and take a deep breath and sit in the driver's seat anyway. And the more you do, the more your confidence will increase.

The word confidence derives from the Latin meaning 'with faith'. So it's not about doing things perfectly well, or making a big splash necessarily. It's about having faith in yourself, trusting that you can deal with whatever life chucks at you. It's about arming yourself with knowledge and preparing yourself as best you can, but ultimately trusting that you know what to do.

Some things I believe about confidence:
- It never goes in a straight line. Your confidence levels will change with time. This is normal;
- The people who appear most confident on the outside are often the most crumbly inside;
- Confidence exists in little pockets throughout your life. The trick is to access the pockets when you need them;
- Children are born with 100% confidence. When did you last see an unconfident newborn baby? Babies don't know enough about the world to be afraid of it, so they have no reason to feel unconfident. You were born confident, therefore you have it within you. It may be buried, but it hasn't gone away and you can find it again.

Ways that you can increase your confidence include:

- Take some exercise. It doesn't much matter what – the point is that you take your focus out of your head and into your body;
- Uplift the externals. New haircut, clothes you love, nice surroundings – all of these things will have a huge effect on how you feel internally. Put it another way – sitting around in a messy house in your oldest jogging trousers with a hole at the knee ain't exactly going to put a whole lot of zipadeedoodah in your day;
- Do something you didn't think people like you did. So if you think of yourself as being fairly intellectual, read a trashy novel. If you think you're quiet, start singing. Challenge your own pre-conceptions of who you really are;
- Talk to a human being. It's terribly retro, I know, but hiding behind email and text messaging doesn't necessarily help your confidence. It might feel like it's keeping you safe, but so much falls through the gaps when you avoid proper conversations;
- Keep a success journal – Even if it's on the back of an envelope, write down your personal successes – the things that made you smile today; the things you're glad you've done; stuff you're proud of having produced. It'll soon add up;
- Do something new and (preferably) slightly scary every day. Today I made a phone call I was avoiding, tomorrow I will eat a papaya etc. That'll stretch your comfort zone pretty fast.

Often the way to increase your driving confidence is to increase your overall confidence, and you don't necessarily need to drive to do that.

**Action points to help you de-stress before driving:**

- Eliminate (or make a plan to eliminate) any obvious stresses from your life;
- Make a plan to bring more calm to your life;
- Do something to relax and calm you every day;
- Create a playlist of music you love;
- Plan your meals so that your blood sugar levels are steady and your caffeine levels are low;
- Practise progressive muscle relaxation, or some other relaxing practice.

**Success story**

*Trisha's story: enjoying driving again*

Trisha went from loving to hating driving and is now making her way back again:

'I learned to drive when I was 17 and loved it. Then some idiot drove into the back of me when I was stopped at a red light and gave me bad whiplash.

I then went off to university and didn't have access to a car for years and I developed a phobia about driving. I even became a very nervous passenger despite doing things like flying an aeroplane solo and a parachute jump.

We moved to a house where I really had no option but to drive, I just forced myself to get on with it and it soon became second nature. I tackled bits of my phobia in stages, first just everyday driving, then getting on a motorway, then driving to places I don't know. I'm still quite nervous of driving somewhere I don't know, I hate being in the wrong lane. Buying a sat nav helped immensely. I realised the other day for the first time since I was 17 (I'm now 35) I had regained my enjoyment of driving.'

# 5. First steps to regaining your driving confidence

Only move on to this stage once you've taken some time to work on your stress levels. This is where regaining your driving confidence really begins in earnest: it's both easy and hard to do. If you don't have a car, now's the time to borrow or arrange access to one. If that's not a possibility, then you may have to cut to the chase and go straight to a driving instructor or professional therapist. Whilst there are things you can do to help before you get in the car, ultimately you will not become a confident driver unless you have access to a car that you can use regularly to practise in.

In this chapter we're looking at:
- How to start becoming more comfortable with your car;
- Can you teach yourself to drive confidently again? Or is the answer simply to go back to basics and take driving lessons again?
- How do you know if you need a driving instructor? And if so, how do you find one?
- What to expect if you take refresher lessons;
- Technical tips to help you drive more confidently.

So where to start if you've never really driven, or haven't done so for a long time?

**Start by sitting in the car**
It's as simple as that– just sit in your car. Or if that's too much, start by opening the car door, then closing it again and walking away. Or just touch it. Simplify this exercise as much as you need to so that you can do it successfully.

Don't turn the key or attempt to drive at all at this point. If you have quite severe anxiety then even this may be difficult for you, but keep telling yourself this – nothing bad can happen if all you are doing is sitting there. You're safe.

And don't be surprised if just sitting there leads to you feeling upset or tearful. It's OK. Let it go.

Take a book or an MP3 player with music you love to listen to into the car (see the chapters on stress and panic attacks for more tips on using music to help keep you calm).

Even better, if you have comedy recordings or a funny book you like, take that. The point of doing this is to get you used to sitting in the car in a calm, happy (rather than anxious) frame of mind. You need to build new associations in your mind – that the car is somewhere you can be and feel relaxed. Practice being in the driver's seat and feeling like you belong there.

Do this repeatedly until you feel calm, no matter how long it takes, whether that's every day for a week, every week for a month or whatever you need. Build up the time that you can happily sit in the car for. Don't even think about driving yet (well, of course you will, but don't think you 'should' be driving just yet). At first you may feel quite anxious and upset to be there – by sitting in your car like this, you are facing up to the fear, and the fear could well have something to say about that.

Many people told me that having a fear of driving can feel like a shameful thing, since it's something that so much of the population appear to do without problems (note that word 'appear' – as we have also already heard, in many instances that's simply not the case).

So with so much riding on it, so much anxiety chasing at your back, this simple act of sitting in the car may be hard for you to do. That's OK. Just wait for those feelings to pass. And they will pass, eventually. Oh you might have to get tough on them, and chase them away with a blast of loud music, but they're going.

Also, don't be surprised if you intend to do this and take a long time getting round to it. You might be reading this thinking

'That sounds good, I'll do it at the weekend' but then you're busy at work or with the kids, or you can't get away or your partner needs the car or blah blah blah. Just know what you're doing when you're making those excuses.

### Get to know your car
You may have deliberately avoided getting up close and personal with your car, as sometimes it's easier to pretend you don't know a thing about cars rather than admit that the real reason you're avoiding it is because you're scared. But it's time to stop hiding behind those excuses now, and becoming truly acquainted with the car you'll be driving is the first step.

We've already taken some time to feel comfortable simply sitting in the car, and now it's time to develop that and have a little play with the machinery as well. Only progress on to this point once you can calmly and comfortably sit in the car. There's no deadline for this so do it as slowly or as quickly as you need to.

So, sit in the car. Take your car's manual with you. Put the seatbelt on. Wiggle the gear stick. Turn the key in the ignition just enough to engage the electrics. Look around you and check that you know how everything works. Particularly play with the buttons you might not use very often, like the hazard lights or fog lamps.

Read the manual, to increase your knowledge of how the car works, and therefore feel more at ease with it. Open up the car bonnet/hood and take a look – what is all that stuff in there anyway? You don't really need to know it all, but it will help if you have a grasp of the basics. You'll feel more of a sense of ownership and control over driving the more you understand what's going on and how the car works.

Think about the basics of car maintenance – what would you do if you had a flat tyre? Can you check the oil level and top it up? What about the fluid levels?

Do you know how to check the tyre pressure? The easiest way to do it is by using a digital air dispenser which you'll find at most garages. Air pressure is important because it helps the brakes to work properly and will make it slightly easier to drive. If your tyres are under-inflated then they'll have less grip, meaning that the distance it takes the car to brake will be longer.

But don't be put off by all this technical stuff – your knowledge may simply extend as far as knowing who to call or what to Google if you have a problem. Ask around to get the name of a trustworthy local mechanic you can call on if the car starts making funny noises. It will help your confidence to know that you have resources like this should you need them, rather than panicking that you won't know what to do if the car breaks down.

**And away we go! (a little, anyway)**
And the next step is to drive forward five inches. That's all – just five inches. Or if that's too much, how about five centimetres? And then the same back again. Just go backwards and forwards in your drive or wherever the car is parked.

Keep doing this until you feel safe and relaxed. If you are worried about the neighbours wondering what you're up to, do it at night. Or get someone to take you to a deserted car park or field and do it there.

After that, do as much as you're comfortable with – if that's round the block, that's great. The important point is to push yourself a little, stretch your comfort zone, but not too much. Take it really, really slowly at first. But keep going – that's how you'll make progress.

If you are already driving but feel fearful about it, still go through the exercise of sitting in the car until you feel calm and relaxed, and getting to know it from a technical point of view. But you can probably manage a little more than five inches, so start by doing the drives you're most comfortable with and build it up from there.

Try driving round an industrial estate at the weekend, or any other empty open space. You may find that the only other traffic is other learner drivers out practising.

Be aware of your grip on the steering wheel – are you hanging on for dear life? That's not how confident drivers behave. Loosen your grip as much as you can whilst still staying in control.

Build up from these tiny movements, and set yourself new goals each week. What these goals are will be unique to you as an individual, but could be:

- Driving backwards and forwards a few feet;
- Driving to the end of your street;
- Driving (or sitting in the car) every other day;
- Going to the local shop and back;
- Driving a route you haven't been on before (it doesn't have to be long, and could be circular and take you straight back home);
- Driving somewhere beautiful and stopping for a picnic. Plan a really lovely picnic with all your favourite foods;
- Driving with music on, if you don't usually do that;
- Saying yes to every opportunity to drive, i.e. if you're going out with your family, don't automatically leave the driving to your spouse;
- Entering and leaving a dual carriageway or motorway;
- Turning right or left, across traffic;
- Parking in a public car park;
- Filling the car up with petrol yourself;
- Parallel parking (start off with a very wide space to practice the technique);
- Driving at night – just take the car out for 10 minutes at midnight.

You could make a list of driving situations and score them out of 10 depending on how scary you find the prospect of them. Keep this list to refer to in coming months and see if your score changes – the trip to the shops that seemed impossible at first may soon start to feel like something you can do.

The major focus here is less on the actual driving and more on how you feel as you drive, particularly how calm you are. What's more important than where you drive is how confident you feel when you do it. And as we discussed in the previous chapter, the more you do it, the more your confidence will grow. You may start off feeling anxious, but this will lessen and hopefully eventually disappear.

So you don't have to set out an enormous plan before you start this (unless you are the sort of person who actively enjoys plans and spreadsheets, in which case go for it). Simply decide each week what your next goal will be, and feel free to stay doing the same thing for a few weeks if you need to. Only plan the next step, and trust that when you've done that, the step after that will appear. Unlike driving you don't need to know the whole route; you just need to keep moving.

Write down your goal and tick it off when you've done it. You may use a computer for most of your writing, or make notes on your phone, but most people seem to find it particularly satisfying to write down this stuff by hand and tick it off with a big flourish – something about doing it that way makes it all feel more real and solid.

The most important factor is that you keep doing something and don't give yourself another gap in driving or let more than a week go by without driving or at least sitting in the car alone. Keep going, keep moving and this is how you'll get there.

Think of this process as being like building up your driving muscles – you wouldn't expect to walk into a gym and pick up the heaviest bar bell, and neither are you likely to achieve success by heading straight for the fastest motorway.

### Don't let other drivers dent your confidence

When you first start driving (or driving again after a gap), you will make mistakes. Of course you will, we all do. And the result of that may be that other drivers honk their horns at you. This can be off-putting and colour your future driving experiences. People may cut in front of you, or show their irritation with rude hand gestures. They don't know what a big deal it is that you're even on the road at all. All you can do is try your best to be a model of how a courteous driver should behave.

Anyone who is angry at your driving will forget about you as soon as they can't see you anymore. It's nothing personal – you just happened to be the person who got in their way. And maybe you did make a mistake, but that's an inevitable part of the learning process.

When I was re-learning to drive again, this would often happen to me. I was careful when it came to things like signaling where I was going. But I was very unconfident when it came to speed and overtaking. This is what tends to annoy other drivers, and would lead to people parping their horns at me. But you just have to let all that stuff wash off you like water off a duck's back. You are not likely to spring immediately out of your phobia and emerge as an ultra confident driver – it's a journey, and we all have to start somewhere. All of that stuff takes time and practise. Eventually you will reach a point where other drivers will have no cause for complaint. That doesn't mean that they won't, because some drivers are aggressive no matter what the situation. But that's their problem – it doesn't have to be yours.

### Expert tip: keep taking small steps

Hypnotherapist Sharon Stiles says that it's important to deal with the negative thoughts to give your positive thoughts about driving a chance to be heard:

'The main thing with any phobia is that it is reinforced by the person constantly running through the negative phobic thoughts. So, they never have any opportunity to spend any time thinking about positive ones. Or if they do they seem so unlikely because they have such a vast experience of all the fearful ones. It's a bit like trying to listen to some pleasant quiet music when there's a jackhammer digging up the road outside. You just can't hear the music because the other sound is too loud. If you can quieten down the negative thoughts then you give the positive thoughts a chance. Hypnotherapy is a good way of doing this because it helps to relax your mind and also helps to address the cause of any fears so that you can put them into context, then let the positive thoughts get stronger.

Taking things in small steps is important too. By constantly achieving things it makes people feel much more confident and so that starts to build up the positive thoughts and they become more real. So, rather than trying to build up courage to drive across town, just drive around the block once, park the car and go back in the house. The next day do the same. When that feels easy, maybe even boring, go round the block twice or go round two blocks. Build up the journeys slowly, always within your limits and your mind will get used to the fact that driving is OK.

It's always good to do everything you can to feel calm before you leave on a journey. That way panic feelings should be minimised. You can also break the journey down into small sections in your mind so that you are only ever driving a short distance at a time.'

## Driving tip: take in the full picture

As your driving confidence improves, widen your focus to take in your surroundings as much as you can. Do this as soon as you can, even if you are only driving a small distance. Is it a lovely sunny day? Or is it cold and rainy, so you're snug and dry in your car? How are you benefiting from this drive? Does it mean you don't have to carry heavy shopping, or your kids can get to where they need to on time? Does it show that you are taking control and moving away from living in the shadow of fear?

Take in everything about the day that there is to appreciate. Make it about more than just the act of driving. Since I drive a Mini, I love spotting other Minis on the roads and shouting 'Hey! Italian Job!'. Unlike me, it never gets old.

It's a distraction technique, but one that has a purpose since it's aiming to take you further towards becoming someone who enjoys driving. As we will see when we look at panic attacks in more detail, distraction is your friend. No, it doesn't deal with the underlying cause, but it gives your feelings a new outlet, and means that fear will not always be your automatic response to driving. Cognitive Therapist Dan Roberts has this advice:

> 'If you feel panic rising, distraction is a key technique to use. Find something you can focus on completely, like the second hand on your watch, or doing a Sudoku puzzle (once you have pulled over, of course!). You could also do simple times tables or just count backwards from 100 to 1 – anything that distracts you from the panicky feelings, because panic attacks are caused by getting anxious about being anxious, so taking your mind of the anxiety will really help.'

**Expert tip: analyse your assumptions**
Dan Roberts adds:

> 'Stress is primarily caused by our unhelpful thoughts and beliefs, so nervous drivers will be thinking things like, "I'm a rubbish driver – I'm bound to have an accident" or "Driving is so dangerous! Everyone else on the road is a lunatic". It's not hard to see how these ideas would make us feel stressed about driving. To feel more confident, try writing down your thoughts about driving in general, you as a driver and other drivers on the road – then ask yourself questions like these about each thought:
> • Is it logical?

- Would a scientist agree with this idea?
- Is there any evidence to support this idea? Or to support a more rational view?
- What would I tell a nervous friend to help calm them down?
- If it's upsetting me, what would be a more helpful way to think?'

### Driving safely whilst feeling severely anxious

In the UK, you need to notify the Drivers and Vehicle Licensing Agency (DVLA) if you have been diagnosed with 'severe anxiety and depression with significant memory and concentration problems, agitation, behavioural disturbance or suicidal thoughts'.

If you do not do this, you will not be able to drive legally and your insurance may not be valid.

You can do this by downloading a medical questionnaire from the DVLA website (details at the back of this book). You will also need to give consent for the DVLA's doctors to contact your doctor.

After investigations, possible outcomes include: being allowed to keep your driving licence; taking your driving licence away; or judging that your medical condition needs to be regularly reviewed and issuing you with a licence that's valid for up to three years. If you disagree with the outcome, you may appeal. The reason for doing this is for your own safety and that of other road users.

I think it's fair to say that anyone with a fear of driving will, by definition, feel anxious about it, so think about whether the DVLA's criteria applies to you. Read through the chapters on panic attacks and stress relief for more tips about how to deal with these feelings. Talk to your doctor if you're unsure about whether your anxiety is severe enough for you to need to inform the DVLA about it. People have their licences removed (and sometimes returned) for all sorts of medical reasons so your GP will be able to give you an informed opinion.

**Don't drive with someone who makes you even more nervous**

One thing you don't need when you're re-connecting with your driving confidence is being put off by someone who undermines it, even if they don't mean to. Lovely and loving as they may be, your nearest and dearest are not necessarily the best people to help you to learn to drive or overcome your fear. If you don't have it, a fear of driving can be hard to understand, so a person who doesn't really get where you're coming from may not be able to show as much patience as you need.

A study in 2011 by Aviva, Britain's largest car insurer, found that over half of women drivers said that having their boyfriend or husband in the car filled them with nervousness and anxiety.

The research also found that nine per cent of men polled refuse to let their girlfriend or wife drive their car. A fifth of this figure said that this is because their partner's driving skills aren't as high as their own. Gee, thanks guys. I think you're pretty perfect too.

Twenty-six per cent said that their car is far too powerful for a female to drive while 16 per cent feel as though their partner displays a lack of confidence whenever driving.

The women polled also had some criticisms as 13 per cent believed their partner is too arrogant while on the road. One in ten said that their partner either drives too fast or is reckless behind the wheel. In comparison, at least 17 per cent of males believe that they are better drivers than their partners and an additional 16 per cent don't think their partner can park a vehicle well enough.

So, to sum up – very few people have confidence in their other half's driving. Is it any wonder so many of us feel undermined as drivers?

Think carefully about who you drive with. If there isn't anyone in your life with the skills to help you, you may be better sticking to the person who understands you best and go it alone. Or it may be time to call in an objective outsider.

**Do you need driving lessons?**

For some people, following the plan set out earlier in this chapter, combined with general stress reduction techniques, will be enough to get them back to driving again. For others it won't, and this is no failure – I think it's more of a failure not to seek out professional help when you need it. If you have been trying to stick to a weekly plan to increase your driving confidence and experience, but for whatever reason it hasn't happened, then it's time to look around for someone who can give you the extra, individual support you need. Not everyone who's overcoming fear of driving will need a driving instructor, so how do you know if this is what you need?

As we've just noted, your mum who squeals every time you speed up, or your partner who's afraid you're going to scratch the paintwork, aren't the right people to be helping you increase your driving confidence. If the person in the car with you is anxious in any way, then it will only increase your anxiety. So a professional, who does this sort of thing day in, day out, and has probably worked with far worse drivers than you, can often be worth their weight in gold.

Where ever you are in the world, driving lessons with a professional instructor are unlikely to be cheap. But in some ways that can be a good psychological push too – you won't want to waste that money, so you'll turn up for the lessons. Actually, you'll have no choice, as the instructor will be outside your house at the time you agreed. So if paying for lessons is a bit of a stretch for you, that's no bad thing.

If you're in the UK, take advantage of a brilliant freebie as the AA (Automobile Association) runs a Drive Confidence course at no charge. At the time of writing they have told me that this course does not have a closing date and is intended to run indefinitely – find out how to book in the resources section at the back of the book.

So, can you do it on your own or will you need help to get driving again? If you don't have a current driving licence then you definitely will. Otherwise, think of it like this:

Consider hiring a driving instructor if:
- You have been trying to return to driving by your own efforts for some months but have not succeeded;
- You are making weekly driving goals but not doing them;
- You always find an excuse not to drive;
- You haven't driven for over a year;
- You do not have a calm and confident driver with whom you feel safe and secure to go out on test drives with;
- You want a professional assessment of your own driving – a driving instructor will be able to give you feedback on your driving style. You may turn out to be a much better driver than you give yourself credit for.

You can design your lessons to suit you – where would you like to drive to? What parts of your locality do you find particularly challenging to negotiate? You can choose to spend an entire lesson entering and leaving a dual carriageway or simply going to the shops and back. The whole point of taking lessons is to support you, so tell your instructor what you need and focus on that. Or you can try out a number of instructors – one recovering driving phobic told me that she found it particularly helpful to have two different driving instructors. This helped her get wider feedback and when they both told her she was a good driver, she started to believe it.

*View from the driving instructor*
Peter Skelton is an experienced driving instructor who's used to nervous drivers and pupils who want to regain their confidence:

> 'People like this are usually much better drivers than they think they are. Often they're not bad drivers at all, and if anything are much better than the 17 year olds who just want to drive fast. People will get particular scenarios in their head, like thinking that they can't do roundabouts or passing. I've had people burst into tears, but we took it steady and eventually they believe they can do it.

Unconfident drivers tend to be much more worried about other drivers, so they'll stare into the middle mirror instead of looking at the road ahead, or pull the clutch up and stall. They'll say things like "I'm really rubbish, I'm the worst driver you have" but it's not true. They just need to be encouraged and guided.'
www.peterskelton.co.uk

*My experience of returning to driving lessons*

The route to my becoming a driver again started through taking around ten driving lessons. People have often asked if I can recommend my driving instructor. But the truth was she had no sort of special training in helping driving phobics like me, and this was what I wanted – to be treated like any other driver, because that's what I wanted to become.

I live in Brighton, a seaside town on the south coast of England with an iconic sea front which has been the star of numerous films and TV shows. On sunny days, many people in the south of England drive down to Brighton beach to take in the sea air.

I started to think that I could, and would, be one of them. I had a vision of myself driving a red Mini along Brighton seafront. At the same time, I was getting bored of living under the shadow of fear. It was no fun at all. But driving a Mini along the seafront – that seemed to promise much more fun.

These thoughts led me to wonder whether taking lessons in a Mini might help. As the fear had begun, so it might end in the same type of car. Well, it was worth a shot. I even went so far as to look up driving instructors in the Yellow Pages and note which ones had Minis. But The Fear stopped me from calling.

Then one day I was walking home and I saw it – a red Mini with a driving instructor's sign on the roof. I quickly took a note of the website address, came home and looked it up. Luckily I was close to home so not much chance to change my mind.

I found the first few lessons to be enormously stressful, almost terrifying. I drove right from the start, which I hadn't done in years. The instructor had no idea how big a deal this was to me. But sometimes that's what you need – if the person with you treats it as no big deal, then you can maybe start to take on those thoughts too.

In between the first three lessons, I couldn't bring myself to get into the car again, so I only drove in the instructor's car. It was a dual control car, and that helped enormously because I knew the instructor could take over at any time. It made the driving feel much safer. I wasn't ready to be in control of a car, so this was a good half-way house. I had someone there to rescue me if the need arose. It was a physical and mental safety net.

But then after a few weeks I pushed myself a little more and drove the family car in between driving lessons – just the once, around the block. Then I set myself the challenge of driving every other day. Not a big drive – it could be just a minute's worth around the corner. It could be just sitting in the car and inching it forward. But every inch was a big achievement.

During our lessons, I asked the instructor to take me out on a few routes that I would like to be able to drive. This is the great thing about being a learner when you already have a driving license – you don't have to go where all the other learners go, ticking off the manoeuvres as you learn them. You can design your lessons to suit yourself. So if all you want is to be able to go to the shops and back, that's fine. I spent a whole lesson going back and forth around a particularly tricky roundabout near my home. For my first lesson, we drove along the sea front.

And yes there were times when I did it all wrong and the in-structor had to grab the wheel or slam down on the dual-control brakes. But there were no crashes, and nobody got hurt.

I had around ten lessons in the end. I didn't make a con-scious decision to stop – they just petered out when the instruc-tor went on holiday. After that the onus was on me to keep up the good work. At this point I honestly thought I'd dealt with the worst of it, and that I'd be sailing along the motorways in no time.

But life, as always, has other plans. It was a long, slow, hard progress, and well over a year before I felt safe enough to venture anywhere near a motorway. I counted off the little milestones and mini victories. Mostly, it was a question of being persistent and never letting more than a week go by without driving, even for a very short distance.

## My milestones

This is how I knew I was making progress:

- Being able to sit in the car without my legs shaking and wanting to run away;
- Sitting in the car and feeling like I was in charge and could decide where to go;
- Driving in between driving lessons (this took me about three weeks to be able to do, so for the first three lessons I was doing no extra practice);
- Offering to drive when we went out as a family;
- Offering to drive when we went out as a family and actually wanting to do it (that took a while);
- Driving to the shops and back, especially an out of the way shop that nobody but me would want to go to;
- Dealing with someone parping their horn at me without wanting to cry and get out of the car;
- Driving without someone parping their horn at me at some point of the journey;
- Driving with music playing – this took about a year; I had to have absolute silence to concentrate before then. Now I think I would just make a better mix CD;
- Singing whilst driving. The soundtrack from *Wicked* was a really wise purchase;
- Driving on a motorway and being able to get up to the speed limit;
- Picking my child up from a play date, so they didn't have to walk miles home in the rain when they were exhausted (this is what used to happen);

- Driving to a job I wouldn't have been able to accept if I hadn't been able to drive to get there;
- Driving at short notice on a motorway in rush hour so I could get to the hospital in time to support my friend who was having her baby.

What could your milestones be? Write some down in your notebook now.

## Do you need a specialist?

There are now driving instructors who specialise in helping people overcome fear of driving. Julian Smith of Ride Drive (a company providing specialist driver training for people with driving phobia) is critical of the standard of driving instructor training in the UK, and feels that this is part of the problem that means that people who pass their test aren't adequately prepared in the first place:

> 'I don't feel that your average driving instructor has any-thing to give your average person with driving phobia, since they will only have been trained in working with novice drivers. Our trainers are specialist traffic police who have much wider experience of all sorts of road conditions.'
> www.ridedrive.co.uk

At the least, you need an instructor who is kind and compassionate, caring and patient. Ask around amongst your friends and family for recommendations and have a chat to a few instructors before you book anything – hire the one you feel most rapport with.

**Driving tip: use a satellite navigation system (sat nav)**

Amongst both professionals who deal with the condition and people with fear of driving, use of a sat nav was the one tip that came up more than anything else as being a helpful thing to do. People really seem to find that they make a big difference. Using a satellite navigation system takes away the fear of getting lost, tells you where you need to go next and means that there's one less part of the driving process for you to think about.

*JD's story*

JD has found that using a sat nav has been a great way to deal with fear of driving.

> 'I am usually a very confident person but I have a lack of confidence behind the wheel. Things came to a head when I had to travel to several appointments over a short space of time. I didn't have time to plan each journey so I had to find a way of overcoming my fear. My solution was to buy a Sat Nav. At last the lovely "lady" on my dashboard became my navigator. I could relax safe in the knowledge that even if I took a wrong turn (Stella as I named her) would not abandon me and would always find a way to my destination.'

If you don't have a sat nav, before you go somewhere new, really study your map and write down places to look out for so that you're more likely to remember. Everywhere you're familiar with driving to now was once a new place, so you can do this.

Use your computer to look at Google street view to see what the place you're driving to actually looks like – this makes it more known than unknown, and hence less scary. Look out for places you might park and plan this element of the journey too.

**Driving tip: keep your distance from the car in front.**

A Canadian survey in 2011 found that one of the biggest annoyances for drivers was people who drive too closely. 39% of people said that they felt anxious when the car behind was too close.

Now, if you are very wrapped up in your own anxiety, you might wonder why you should be worrying about other people's fears too. But if you want to make the roads calmer – both for yourself and for other road users – then this is one way to do it. So watch out for times when you might be getting too close to the car in front and potentially annoying that driver. Confident drivers don't set out to annoy others. So stay confident, and stay back.

**Driving tip: keep your speed up**

When people are nervous drivers, they inevitably drive cautiously, which often leads to slowing down. It may feel safer to you to be at 40mph even if the speed limit will let you do 60mph.

However, by driving slowly you are actually making driving conditions less safe for yourself, since slow drivers are another major irritant for other road users. So if you're irritating the drivers around you, they're more likely to beep their horns, try to get past you or drive aggressively – all of which may end up making you feel more nervous.

A study in 2011 revealed that 60% of motorists experience an increase in stress levels and a heightened irritability when faced with a vehicle driving slower than the rest of the traffic. The Department of Transport also found that nearly 150 accidents per year are directly caused by slow driving. There have even been calls to introduce a 'slow speed camera' or a dedicated 'slow lane'.

The message to take from this is not to simply speed up regardless, but to be aware of the speed limits wherever you're driving and aim to keep up to them. Even though you probably can't help it, slowing down the traffic will annoy other drivers and make your journey less safe, as you are then disrupting the natural flow of the traffic.

Make it part of researching your journey to know what the speed limits are on the roads you intend to drive, and aim to stick to them. It's safer to do so.

### Driving tip: dealing with tailgating

Even if you do this well, given that there are so many anxious (or just plain impatient) drivers on the road, it's possible that though you may be keeping your speed up and staying a good distance from the car in front, the car behind you may decide to get too close for comfort.

Don't allow this to panic you or take it personally – it is the driver behind's responsibility to hold back and leave a safe stopping distance between their car and yours. Check your speedometer and as long as you are driving at the appropriate speed limit then you don't need to speed up (though it may feel like the driver behind wants you to). Use your own judgement – you may be able to see something on the road ahead which the driver behind can't. Or perhaps the person behind is indicating that they're intending to overtake, in which case, again, it's their responsibility to do so safely.

Of course that doesn't mean that they will, and you will meet people who drive aggressively where ever you are. That's their problem, don't make it yours. You can only keep yourself calm. So let them pass if they want to.

### Become confident by modelling yourself on a confident driver

If we are to become fully confident drivers ourselves, it really helps if you have someone you can model yourself on.

If you simply don't know how to be a confident driver, look around amongst your friends and family to find someone who is. Not an arrogant or reckless driver, but someone who's quietly confident about it all. Take a drive with them and notice what they do, and how they behave. How is that different to how you behave?

When I was starting to drive again, my instructor pointed something out. As I was pulling out at a junction, I would of course check both ways to ensure that no traffic was coming and that it was safe to pull out. Then I would check again. And again. And again. My head was spinning to left and right so fast, it looked like there was a high speed tennis match taking place.

I thought that this was a safe thing to do – to check and check again. Because my fear-sodden brain was telling me 'even though you've checked that there are no cars coming, there still might be. Just because you can't see a car, doesn't mean there isn't one just out of sight preparing to roar up the road and smash into your door.' Fear never was one to win points for rationality.

Except, as my driving instructor pointed out, this isn't how a confident driver behaves. They check, trust themselves that they now know when it's safe to move out, then do so. And it's impractical too – by the time you've faffed about checking and re-checking several times, the road that was safe to drive out on to when you started may well have filled up with traffic again.

So it may be worth asking yourself – what driving habits have you picked up that are really all about your fear? Is this really how a confident driver would behave? What would you be doing differently if you felt at 100% confidence?

## The confident driver's story

Amongst our stories of people with experience of fear of driving, I thought it would be helpful to hear from someone who has never felt any such thing.

### Judith's story

Judith Morgan is one such confident driver, who regards it with energy and excitement. So how does she manage that?

'What do I like about driving? My enjoyment of it and the benefits it brings to my life. I think I found it very liberating as a younger woman so effectively it meant I could please myself about what I wanted to do and when, and not be dependent on anyone else.

I had to take three tests before I passed. And that night my parents took me into Richmond Park in their Volvo Estate. The whole experience went so badly that I didn't drive again for six years, until I realised how ridiculous this was at age 23. I looked around me and said to myself "if all these other muppets can do it, then so can I". Had six refresher lessons, bought a Mini Metro and never looked back.

My mum also loved to drive. I think she loved all the things I describe about freedom, independence etc. She also rode motorbikes and drove cars for a motor auction. She later did some chauffeuring with a long wheelbase limo and also worked for a Rolls Royce franchise. She just loved driving and cars, and lusted after fast cars in particular and would discuss these in the car when we were children. Definitely a good driving role model.'

It's interesting how Judith has had some of the experiences that can contribute towards a driving phobia. But she was not stressed at this time, and in any case had a very good pro-driving role model in the figure of her mother. Imagine the difference it would make to your children if you had a more positive attitude to driving. Or if you were an example to them of how not to let fear squash you down or run your life. That's the kind of role model I want to be to my kids.


## Can you ever, truly get rid of a phobia like this?

In truth, some experts think not – it's more a case of accepting what you've got, and learning to manage it. It may never go away

100%, and may decide to reassert itself at inconvenient times. But that doesn't mean it's beaten you.

Nowadays, I think of my recovered driving phobia as being like a scar that I've learned to live with. It's a place on the map of my life. It's not everything I am, and overcoming it was an achievement. I don't deny that it's there, or was there, but I'm moving far beyond it now.

## Obstacles to becoming a confident driver

I think one of the hardest things for the fearful driver to deal with are the times when you know you haven't driven as well as you could, and perhaps someone beeps their horn or gets angry on the road with you. Bear in mind that people will sound their horns for all sorts of reasons, many of them nothing to do with you. Don't feel you have to be responsible for someone else's frustration. There's not a lot you can do about it if someone is prone to being an angry driver, other than not taking it personally.

But if someone does beep their horn, ask yourself – do they have a point? Was I driving too slowly, not indicating properly or doing something that might give other drivers just cause to complain?

And crucially – what do I need to do differently next time? Use the experience as a learning opportunity, not as a chance to blame yourself or reinforce your belief that you're not a good driver. If anything, you have the potential to be one of the best drivers on the road, because you don't take it for granted and are always focused on keeping safe.

## Success story

*Lucy's story – sheer determination not to be isolated*
Journalist Lucy Jolin is a 37-year old mother of two, and someone who slipped from being an unconfident driver, into a non-driver,

but has now bounced back. In her case, it was a series of accidents that prompted the fear:

> 'It took me six attempts to pass my test. That knocked my confidence to start with.
>
> Then a few years later, I was involved in an accident – I wasn't driving, my husband was. He was sensible and got straight back in a car as soon as possible. I didn't. By then I was married and I let the fear build up because, well, I could. He was happy to drive, so I just never drove. Before long, I found that I actually couldn't drive.
>
> This situation went on until I had my first child. He had jaundice and after he came out of hospital he needed to go back every two days for blood tests. I couldn't afford to get taxis all the time and so the only option I had to get my baby to the hospital was to drive. It was utterly terrifying the first time. There was a particularly nasty roundabout which I was really scared of. I made my husband write down the exact route which I memorised. I did it because I had to do it, there was no other option.
>
> Then I thought to myself: if I don't drive with a child, I'm going to be so isolated. So I told my husband that from now on, I was going to do all the driving until I got over my fear. He was quite surprised but said fine, and he was brilliant. He never said anything to undermine me or make me nervous and I stuck to it: I think I drove absolutely everywhere for at least a year. Into Central London, up to Scotland, everywhere. And it worked! Now I can drive anywhere without fear. I look back and I'm amazed that I let it go on as long as I did. I now like driving. I probably do it more than my husband ever did. I can go anywhere I like with the kids and am honestly not afraid in the slightest.'

# 6. Dealing with anxiety and panic attacks

In this chapter we're looking at one of the most common, frightening and physical symptoms of driving anxiety – the panic attack.

You don't have to have a phobia to experience a panic attack, but many people say that it's been the experience of having a panic attack whilst driving which has put them off driving in the future. And if you do experience one, you'll know all about it.

So in this chapter we're looking at panic attacks in the context of driving:

- What causes panic attacks and how do I know if I'm having one?
- Does having a panic attack mean that there's something serious wrong with me?
- What's the best way to deal with panic attacks whilst driving?
- What should I do if I am out in traffic and start to have a panic attack?
- How can I stop panic attacks from happening in the first place?

The aim of this chapter is to help you feel more in control of your reactions, and to give you practical tools to help stop panic attacks from happening in the first place, and to deal with them should one occur.

As we have noted from the start, there are many shades of fear of driving, but if you are experiencing panic attacks then it's safe to say that you are at the more serious end of the scale and are more likely to need professional help to overcome this.

Of course, equally you may not – I got over my driving related panic attacks by myself (with a little help from a driving instructor) and have spoken to others who have done the same. But if you're looking for an indicator into how bad you've got it – this could be it.

Panic attacks, like fear of driving itself, are more common than you think. So if you're assuming that it's only you that feels like that – really, the truth is that it's you and several million others. Only it's not something we advertise or talk about particularly openly.

But that's changing. I think people are starting to talk about panic attacks more now because they can do so in an anonymous way, especially via blogs, forums or a social media persona. I've listed some of these in the resources section at the back of the book . So if you can, do talk about it. Just because you feel alone with this doesn't mean that you are

## What is a panic attack?

If you've had one you'll know that a panic attack is a horrible, horrible thing. Sufferers often genuinely believe that they are having a heart attack or about to die. An attack can seem to come out of nowhere, heralded by physical shakes and an overwhelming feeling of fear. If you are prone to driving anxiety, you may be prone to panic attacks in other situations as well.

For some people, experiencing a panic attack whilst driving is what triggers their phobia in the first place. The brain then continues to associate driving with this fear, and the panic attack becomes a learned response. The good news is that there is quite a lot you can do to manage panic attacks and stop them happening, or head them off if you feel one starting.

## What's happening in your body when you have a panic attack?

The symptoms of a panic attack are very physical and can feel very frightening. Symptoms can include any combination of the following:

- Raised heartbeat – you may feel as if your heart is beating faster than normal, even pounding;
- Churning stomach;
- Sweating, feeling hot, or possibly the opposite and feeling cold;
- Physical trembling and shaking, particularly in the legs or arms;
- Feeling short of breath, as if you can't really breathe properly;
- Discomfort around your chest, or feeling nauseous;
- Feeling dizzy, as if you may faint;
- Numbness or tingling sensation.

You may fear that you're having a heart attack, or be about to do something irrational such as turn the car out into oncoming traffic. Time may appear to speed up or slow down. If you were to describe panic attacks in a work of fiction, no one would believe you. You might as well refer to them as an 'Attack of the Flying Dingbats'. Actually, let's do that

Now who could really be expected to drive through that lot? Not me, that's for sure.

Typically, a full blown panic attack may be over in 10 minutes, whilst a mini-attack may last for even less than that. But even once these physical symptoms have passed, you may continue to feel ill at ease for much longer. To put it bluntly, a panic attack can leave you feeling like crap for hours.

Whilst these symptoms disappear quickly and do not generally signal that anything serious is physically wrong with you, if you have experienced one or more panic attacks then it's important to see your doctor to officially rule out anything more serious. Chances are that you're physically fine. It's all a cruel trick of the mind. Your health may be great, it's just your mind that's under attack from those blasted Flying Dingbats.

## What causes this?

Some studies suggest that women are up to three times more likely to experience panic attacks than men. Or is it just that women are happier to admit to them? For women who have a history of them, panic attacks can also increase during pregnancy.

The American Psychological Association has estimated that one in 75 people in the US experience panic attacks. So, whilst it's not totally commonplace, neither is it exactly rare. Panic attacks have been, or will be experienced by millions of people around the world.

The exact causes of panic attacks are not known, but suspected causes include: behaviour of the amygdala (a part of the brain); the actions of serotonin, a brain chemical; and your learned responses to stressful situations

Researchers are undecided as to whether biological, psychological or even genetic causes are to blame for panic attacks. These attacks are no real respecter of who you are – people in the public eye can suffer just as much as people who never leave the house.

Some writers on the subject feel that creative, imaginative people are more prone to panic attacks, perhaps because their brains are more wired to create something that's not there. A creative mind can conjure up some good stuff, but it's also pretty good at bringing up the bad stuff as well.

Years before I ever had a driving phobia, I had two panic attacks, months apart. Both were in public places and led to an ambulance being called to take me to hospital. But once I got to the emergency room, after a cursory check the doctors pretty much shrugged their shoulders and sent me on my way home. Like colic in babies, panic attacks may look and feel dramatic, but to the medical profession they're fairly ordinary and no biggie at all. So whilst it is recommended that you get your panic attacks checked out by a doctor, this is purely precautionary and likely to be treated in a low level way – you won't be getting rushed into the emergency room just yet.

## The fight or flight response

Most commonly, panic attacks are associated with the behaviour of the amygdala, a small part of the brain which triggers the 'fight or flight' response – preparing the body to either combat or run away from a dangerous or stressful event. It's a self-protection mechanism as your body prepares to guard you from danger. So you can see how this could be triggered if you've started to regard driving as dangerous or stressful, and how this can happen more easily if you have not been driving for a while or have been involved in a crash or negative driving incident. Your body has learned that driving is a perilous situation, and so the fight or flight response is triggered to protect you – the irony being that it actually ends up doing the opposite.

What's happening here is that your body is sensing imminent danger, and producing large quantities of adrenaline to help deal with this. This might have been useful in ancient times, if you were a cave dweller who needed to fight off a wild beast. But today? Not so much. Somebody tell that to our brains please. I mean, it's great that the body has some sort of self-preservation survival mode, but you'd think that by now it would have realised that sometimes this produces the opposite effect and leads to people thinking that they're going to die rather than survive. These days, we rarely actually need to fight or flight, (and especially not when we're driving), it's just that our minds haven't quite cottoned on to the fact yet. So a big part of dealing with this phobia is to stop this reaction from being triggered.

## Dealing with panic attacks: take control by tracking how they start

The first step in dealing with panic attacks is to learn to recognise which physical symptoms signal the start of one for you. Look for the early twinges, because if you get a handle on these then you will be able to head off your panic attacks before they even get going.

After you've had one (or thinking about the last one you can remember), write down:

- How you felt beforehand,
- How did you know it was beginning? What were the physical symptoms?
- What was happening just before that?
- What could you have done differently?
- How would you handle this next time?
- What could you do differently next time?

I know you won't feel like doing this if you've just had a panic attack – you'll probably feel more like crawling into a dark space until your body feels a bit more normal, but it's a crucial exercise to do.

By picking apart and analysing your own panic attacks like this, you're less of a victim and more in control. It becomes less of a thing that's happening to your body, and more of an event that you can start to manage.

For me, panic attacks start with a 'rising' sensation in my stomach and slightly shaking hands. Often the simple act of noticing symptoms like this can help a lot, as it takes you outside yourself to note them as an objective observer, rather than staying as a victim within them.

And it's important to get across that you can stop them – the beginnings of a panic attack do not always have to become The Real Deal. Once you get to know your own panic attacks, then you are in a much better place to deal with them – you'll know when you have felt one or two of your symptoms starting, and that you need to take action such as relaxation or distraction exercises as described in this chapter to stop it developing further.

## Panic attacks whilst driving

As we've seen in previous chapters, many people who are afraid to drive still find they have to do it anyway. And the trouble with panic attacks is that they have an extremely poor sense of timing. So what should you do if you're out on the road and you feel the risings of a panic attack? How can you calm yourself down again and continue with your journey? How can you ensure that this doesn't keep becoming your learned response to driving?

When I started driving again after a seven year gap, I always knew when I had pushed myself too far. A familiar rising panic would begin, and my hands and legs might shake slightly. Sometimes the rising was only like a small hillock, and I'd pass over it within seconds. If I could grit my teeth and get through that horrible, brief time, then I was generally OK for the rest of the drive. So that's one way to deal with mini-panics – literally sit it out, and trust that it will pass.

However, sometimes the panic would rise up to mountainous proportions, and I would have to pull over and get out of the car. This led to a few hairy moments on the hard shoulder, but ultimately it was probably safer to hand over the steering wheel to my partner at that point. So that's another way to deal with panic attacks – stop what you're doing and delegate. Of course it doesn't really deal with the root cause, but ultimately you have to do what's safest for other road users and yourself. So if you're prone to panic attacks, think before you drive – what's your plan of action going to be?

I think a panic attack whilst you're driving is a doubly-frightening experience. It's bad enough if your body starts to shake involuntarily, but what if you're meant to be in charge of a car at the same time? What if there are passengers you're supposed to be keeping safe as well?

**Be prepared**
There are lots of practical ideas in this chapter for things you can do to prevent and deal with panic attacks so read all of this carefully and get prepared. You may never need to put your preparations into action, but it's much better to have the peace of mind of knowing that you can deal with this.

And if you have a history of panic attacks whilst driving, make a point of doing some of the relaxation exercises described in this chapter any time you're paused in traffic, to stop the stress from building up.

## Expert tip: positive self-talk

Dr Rick Norris advises that if you feel overwhelmed by panic when you're driving, stopping and talking yourself back to positivity can be done:

'Stop in a safe place, open the window and start to breathe quickly and shallowly (panting). Some people find it helpful to get out of the car and walk about. Positive self talk, out loud if necessary, can help. "Come on Rick, you know you can do this, you've done it loads of time before."

Then when restarting your drive be very conscious about what you are doing. The harder you concentrate on the driving actions the less room in your mind for negative thoughts. And again talk yourself through it out loud. "I'm turning on the engine and checking my mirror, I'm putting it into first gear I can see it's safe and I'm pulling away. Well done Rick, you're doing okay. I'm taking second gear and I'm moving ok, I'm coping with the other traffic, I can do this. I can see I have to turn left at the end of the road so I know what I have to do."

Identifying the source of the fear or panic can help to decide what we need to do specifically. So, for example, if it's fear of getting lost then sat navs can make a world of difference as many people now worry much less about getting lost, although they seem to panic if they haven't got sat nav to rely on once they become used to it.'

**Expert tip – Steer, don't brake**

Mike Rees is Managing Director of Drive Alive UK Ltd, a company specialising in driver safety training. He has witnessed people having panic attacks whilst driving and this is his advice:

- Try to remain calm, panic is your worst enemy;
- Relax the grip on the steering wheel, focus on the road ahead and lift off the accelerator in order to create some space around the vehicle;
- DO NOT HIT THE BRAKES;
- Move to the left and pull off the road in a safe place;
- Stay behind the wheel for some minutes and breathe until you feel calmer;
- Step out of the car, seek a refuge and give yourself time to relax;
- Only get back behind the wheel if you feel you have regained some composure;
- Try to identify, in these quieter moments, the cause of your reaction.

www.drivealive.co.uk

**Reassurance is your friend**

As Dr Norris has mentioned, reassuring yourself that everything is going to be OK and that this will pass, is one of the most effective things you can do. It might sound obvious, but when you're starting to panic then logic and rationality can fly out the window. Sometimes the best thing you can do is to say out loud 'I'm OK'. Although it might feel like you're going to die, you won't. You might suspect that you're having a heart attack, but you're not.

Speak it out loud and focus on the positive. Take a moment to think about this now and plan how you'll do it in advance. What will your positive, reassuring thought be? For example, telling yourself 'It's OK, I'm not going to die' is not particularly reassuring because in your panicked state, your brain is more likely to pick up on the word die and magnify it until it becomes a big fat DIIIEEEE. And that's not helpful, not at all.

So the type of reassuring message (a bit like the positive mantras we discussed in the chapter on stress) that will help is something that focuses on the positive in a simple and easy way, such as:

I'm OK, I can talk, I can breathe.
Everything's fine.
I'm calm.

Or simply repeat to yourself:
Breathe, breathe, breathe.

Or my personal favourite:
Calm, calm, calm.


**Relax and it will soon be over**

Relaxation exercises will also help you get through panic attacks, though they can be challenging if you're also having trouble with your breathing. Your main aim with this is to focus on keeping your heart rate steady so it can't send all that excess adrenaline coursing through your body.

Slow your breathing down – take big breaths in through your nose and let them out through your mouth as slowly as possible. As you breathe in and your lungs fill, your stomach should go right out – you'll notice this, as it's a deeper breath than normal. When you exhale, your stomach should go back in. In theory it's better if you can do this lying flat or standing up – not normally known as the best positions for driving in. So you may not get the optimum benefit from this exercise if you do it when you're driving, but you'll definitely derive some benefit, and that makes it worth doing.

**Expert tip: breathe**

Hypnotherapist Barbara Ford-Hammond says breathing is the key to dealing with panic attacks:

> 'Remember to breathe. Breath holding or over breathing can set off panic at an alarming rate.
>
> Pull over if it's safe to do so and get a grip before driving again. Say to yourself, "I can do this". "This will pass". "I have control". Or repeat your chosen mantra.
>
> Know that you can change, recover and enjoy driving'.

Cognitive Therapist Dan Roberts also advises deep breathing, four counts in and out:

> 'One technique that is helpful for both stress and panic attacks is deep abdominal breathing, because in both cases the stress response is being triggered, which involves fast, shallow chest breathing from the upper lungs. Instead, consciously slow your breathing right down to a slow count of four in through the nose, then a slow four out through the mouth. Try to completely fill your lungs on each in-breath, then empty them on the out-breath, feeling your abdomen rise and fall as you breathe. Keep this up for anything from a few breaths to a few minutes, until you feel calmer.'

**Relax your muscles**

All of the physical exercises described here can be done as you're driving, and it's a good idea to get in the habit of doing at least some of them regularly, as they will help you stay relaxed and stop too much tension from building up and tipping you over into a panic attack.

1. It can be very helpful to simply shake your arms and legs to get rid of the trembles and help the muscles to relax. You may have to pull over to do this. Or if you pull up at a stop

sign, take advantage of the fact to take your feet off the pedals and wriggle your feet around a bit to help them relax.

2. Progressively tense then relax your muscles as much as you can – draw them in then let them go. As you're holding the steering wheel grip it and then relax – again best done when you're waiting at traffic lights. Keep an eye on your grip generally and make sure it doesn't become too tight without you noticing.

3. Move your shoulders around in circles to relax them – you should be able to do this whilst still holding the car wheel steady. Neck and shoulder muscles can get particularly knotted up if you're driving in an anxious state, so it helps to do this sporadically even if you're not having a panic attack.

4. Move your jaw and face around, as these are areas where stress can easily build up without you realising until it's too late. The good thing about doing this whilst driving is that nobody can see you apart from the rear view mirror, so you're unlikely to attract comments about the fact that you're making funny faces. Another way to do this is by chewing gum whilst you're driving – this works on two levels as it gives you something else to focus on and forces your jaw to keep moving.

### The importance of the food you eat and how it affects you physically

The symptoms of hypoglycaemia (or low blood sugar) can be similar to those of a panic attack, particularly the physical shakes and altered moods. So this is something to think about when you're tracking your attacks – how long was it since your last meal?

If you think that low blood sugar is contributing to your panic attacks, then this is fairly easy to address by eating healthy snacks more regularly to keep your blood sugar levels steady. Don't set off for a drive on an empty stomach. Keep a few cereal bars in the car for emergencies.

The symptoms of hyperglycaemia (high blood sugar) also have something in common with panic attacks, particularly the sensation of tingling in the feet. This is why you will need to have your panic attacks investigated by a doctor, in case they're not panic attacks at all, but rather something else altogether.

## Caffeine and panic attacks

There is no 100% concrete proof that caffeine contributes to anxiety levels and panic attacks, but many experts believe that it does – the American Psychiatric Association recognises caffeine-induced anxiety disorder as a legitimate condition. Caffeine affects people in different ways depending on body size and tolerance levels. And it's important to remember that caffeine doesn't just mean coffee – it's also present in some cola and energy drinks, chocolate and medicines too.

So could it be contributing to your anxiety? Note how you feel after a cup of coffee (or two) and what the difference is. You may be one of those people who's more susceptible to the effects of caffeine than others. If you have a panic attack, think about what your caffeine levels were at that time and whether it may have been a contributing factor.

I definitely noticed that coffee could give me the jitters, so when I was addressing my panic attacks I decided to limit it. So now, I look at it in the wider context of my day. If I know that I am doing something with the potential to be stressful, then I will lay off the caffeine and maybe only have one cup of coffee, first thing in the morning, on that day. If it was potentially an extra stressful day, such as driving to a public speaking engagement in a place I didn't know (double yikes! Did I mention I don't like public speaking either?), then I would probably have no coffee at all on that day, and avoid things like cola or chocolate as well.

Paying attention to diet helped a lot with my panic attacks, especially once I started limiting caffeine and watching out for sugar crashes. I came to learn that setting off after two espressos and no breakfast was a bad, bad idea. So now it's no more than one cup of coffee, and something with a low glyceamic index such as porridge or oat cakes to keep my sugar levels steady. It seems to work.

And if you're feeling tired and need to drive, the best thing you can do is to take a drink of cold water rather than a hot coffee to wake you up.

## Expert advice: the positives and negatives of caffeine

Registered nutritionist Dr Carina Norris says that caffeine is a double-edged sword when it comes to anxiety and driving:

'A cup of coffee may increase your alertness – making you feel "on top of your game" – and increasing your self-confidence. In this case it may be a good idea to have a cup before a lesson, or particularly before your driving test.

However, too much caffeine can make you feel shaky, jittery and extremely anxious and the level at which you hit too much varies a lot. A large part of our sensitivity to caffeine is genetically determined. So some of us find that coffee in moderation provides a welcome boost, while for others, even a single cup can send us into a jittery mess! You really need to get to know how your body reacts to caffeine, to work out whether it's a help or a hindrance, and how much is a good idea to take. Also, our bodies become habituated to coffee's effects. If you only drink it occasionally, a cup will give you far more of a buzz than if you drink it every day.

So, to sum up, caffeine can help you feel alert, but there's a fine line between this and feeling jittery, and you have to find out where this line lies – for you.

Also, remember that the caffeine content of coffee shop coffees varies a lot. And also that smaller amounts of caffeine is contained in other drinks, such as cola and tea, and in some painkillers and cold remedies.'

**Expert tip: eat something cold**

Anxiety expert Charles Linden has a practical approach:

> 'There are a couple of "first aid" devices that can be help-
> ful during the onset of a panic attack. Slowly eat a cold
> apple or two and drink cold water to activate the "dive
> refle" which causes the heart rate and breathing to slow
> down. Use my Panic Attack Eliminator App from iTunes
> which talks you through how to deactivate a panic attack.
>
> It is also useful to use diversion, so mind games like
> counting objects as you pass them or playing word games
> in the head are useful... if all else fails, try turning on some
> loud music and sing along to deactivate the anxiety re-
> sponse.'

When you eat something cold, essentially what you're doing is distracting your senses so that they must naturally divert away from your anxiety. As Charles Linden mentions, an apple or a bottle of water can be a good choice, or you could go for a packet of mints, a lollypop or sharp tasting sweets. I find that really strong mints, the sort that make you take a sharp intake of breath, are a great help when driving.

Obviously this is something you need to prepare ahead for – rummaging around for sweets definitely isn't going to help you drive more safely. But you could have something to hand in your shirt pocket, on the passenger seat or in the pocket of the car door. If you're driving with a passenger it's even easier to get them primed with something to feed you.

**Stopping a panic attack**

Therapist Phil Parker recognises that stopping a panic attack once it's started is challenging, but it can be done:

> 'Adequate preparation is the best option here. Trying to
> calm a panic attack once it has started without being famil-

iar with the right tools is possible, but it's quite a tall order. So if you've been experiencing panic attacks then seek out one of the practitioners mentioned above, and consider reading the book *Dû- unlock your full potential with a word*. It covers a whole new way of thinking about and dealing with situations where we feel out of control, including panic attacks.

If you've not got the tools yet, then consider first aid for panic attacks:

- Breathe slower;
- Slow down the voice in your head;
- Calmly focus on just one thing at a time;
- Focus on your breathing;
- The things you can see in front of you;
- The slowing down of the voice in your head.

Calmly tell yourself; "this is normal, bit by bit I am calming down, I am coming back to being my old self, I can do this". Avoid negatives such as "I don't want to pass out or get upset".'

## Expert tip: relax before you drive

Harley Street hypnotherapist Dominic Knight says:

'It is now proven that five minutes of heightened anxiety can reside in the nervous system for up to six hours. That's why people experience panic attacks seemingly out of the blue. It's a backlog negative emotion.

Hence it is always important if you do suffer from anxiety that before you drive you sit back and relax as deeply as you can, breathing in for four seconds, holding your breath for eight seconds, then exhaling for 16 seconds. This helps stop the mind racing with thoughts. Then imagine the journey ahead going really well. As you head to the car speak to yourself with an encouraging voice.'

## Using music to distract you

Music can be a fantastic help if you're starting to feel the anxiety rise, because it takes you to an entirely different place emotionally.

Think about the music you play in your car and make a special CD or playlist just for driving. Aim to include only songs you love – perhaps from a time in your life when you felt more confident. It could be songs you've not played in a while, stuff you loved when you were a teenager or your favourite band's greatest hits. If it puts a smile on your face then you need it there in the car with you.

It took me a long time to be able to drive whilst music was playing – I found it incredibly distracting, when all I wanted to do was concentrate on the road ahead. But now I love it and find it very useful. I tend to stay tuned to the local cheesy pop radio station – all the songs are familiar and therefore comforting. It's the kind of station that would make cooler people grind their teeth, but for my purposes, it's perfect. It plays a lot of oldies and well known chart hits, so my attention is drawn by a combination of 'Great – I haven't heard that one in a long time' to 'Oh no, why are they playing that old piece of crap' and then interspacing this with singing along.

My family have learned to live with my terrible singing, as it's substantially better than when I used to freak out and have to stop the car.

*Michael's story*
Michael has now overcome his driving anxiety, and found that music was an enormously helpful tool in supporting him to be a calmer driver.

'Personally, I've found listening to music to be one of the most effective ways of ensuring a calmer drive. Having something to listen to seems to distract the part of my brain that is not involved in driving. This part of the brain can fret, worry, and generally become unnecessarily anxious when I drive. The right choice of music, however, can take its attention and keep it too busy to create any unwanted anxiety. Or at least, that's how it seems to work for me.

The right choice of music is very important, however. Fast, banging dance music is no good at all, especially when the BPM or speed of the track is noticeably faster than your heartbeat. I find driving to music like this extremely stressful, which means that there are many radio stations I can't listen to.

You also have to choose music that you are familiar with, but which you still find interesting enough to keep your attention. Listening to new music is a very different mental process to listening to familiar music, and in terms of preventing driving anxiety it is listening to familiar music which works better for me. Going back to albums that you bought a few years ago, but haven't listened to much since, can be very fruitful.

And finally, you need enough music to make it through long journeys. If you have to keep repeating songs you will eventually get bored of them, and they will no longer distract that troublesome part of your mind. I've found that car CD players that play MP3 CDs are very good for this, as you can put well over 100 songs on one CD in MP3 format. Alternatively, you can make a lengthy driving playlist on an MP3 player. Keeping the play order set to random can help keep things interesting too.'

And if music's really not your thing, you can still use audio to distract your mind in other ways, perhaps by listening to an audio book or an educational CD. If your mind is engaged in learning French, there's less space for the Flying Dingbats to attack.

*Action point: make music now*
Using the pointers above, make yourself a 'Driving Music' CD or playlist. Even if you are pretty far off being able to drive, one day

you will, so get ready for that day. Dig deep into your musical history and rediscover the songs you loved but haven't played in a while. How fun would it be to cruise along listening to that for a while?

### Other distraction techniques

Distraction is your friend and ally in this. The more you can distract yourself from panicky feelings, the better your chances of not being ambushed by them. But if your music player's not working, or you've forgotten to bring your CD, there are still plenty of other things you can do:

- Notice the cars around you. Pick a colour and start to count how many cars of that colour you see;
- Add up the number plates of the cars in front, or look for patterns of recurring numbers;
- Pick out number plates and make up a funny sentence from the letters;
- Talk to yourself – but keep it positive;
- Fantasise – your best ever Christmas, maybe an upcoming event or something you're looking forward to. Think about your favourite star – what would you say to them if they were in the car with you?
- Pretend you've won the lottery – what would you spend your winnings on?

Plan your distraction of choice now, before you need it. What would you do if you started to feel panic rising? Which of these distraction techniques appeals to you most? You'll find it easier to reach for one of these tools if you've already decided what you want to do.

And better still – start to use these distraction techniques when you're driving even if you don't feel especially panicky. They'll help you feel calm.

*Nicky's story*
Nicky Taylor is a 46-year old TV director who has found a number of ways to deal with panic attacks whilst driving:

> 'My fear of driving started 13 years ago. It was especially bad if I hadn't eaten very much (dieting) combined with tiredness.
>
> If I feel a panic attack coming on, I breathe deeply and create anagrams, words from the number plates of cars – the distraction from the fear really works. My kids help here too – they entertain me! We sing very badly in harmony and in rounds, play I spy etc. Distraction and concentrating on something completely different seems to work for me.
>
> The situation has improved now. I can still have a panic attack when I am least expecting it. Factors such as enough sleep and food are key and also the imperative nature of where I am going. The more desperate it is that I have to get there, on time – the more likely it is that I suffer a panic attack. If it's a jolly, non essential journey, I'm not so stressed and I don't have an attack.'

So although Nicky hasn't been able to 100% eliminate her panic attacks, she has developed enough of an understanding of what causes them that she can take appropriate action to minimise them.


## Climb every mountain (road)
Nobody sets out on a car journey planning to have a panic attack. Sometimes they just swoop in when you least expect it. Maybe you've been having panic free drives for ages, when one final attack pops back in to nip you in the butt.

No matter. It's unfortunate, but these things happen. It doesn't mean you've failed. And don't you dare give up on me now.

**What if it all goes wrong?**
So you took all the advice above, and you had your music and your apple and all the rest of it, and still your legs started shaking uncontrollably and you had to give up. That's OK, in fact it's fairly normal. I warned you that this road would be long, and I never promised it was going to be straight.

Do an analysis, just as you did when you were starting to get on top of your panic attacks – what do you think was really going on this time? Had you had too much coffee, or not enough to eat? Or are the underlying stresses in your life still there? It's not like they are going to just evaporate if you don't address them. It's like when you squeeze a balloon – the middle might go in, but the rest of it will still expand, because the same amount of air's still in there.

In any case, feel good that you had a go rather than bad because it didn't work out. Take your next journey as soon as you possibly can, even if it's only to drive for a very short way. This bit will be tough, but it's very necessary. If you need to, go back to the steps in Chapter 5 and just sit there in your car until the feeling passes and you can get into a good mental space.

You tried and it didn't work, but that just means that you are going to try again. You are more than the sum of your panic attacks, and they are not going to beat you.

**Pre-driving checklist:**
- Relax – do deep breathing or muscle relaxation exercises as described above;
- Music, audio book or language CD ready;
- Ensure you're not hungry – eat a healthy snack;
- Put some mints in your pocket or easily at hand;
- Limit caffeine;
- Focus on why you're making this journey – what's the destination? (rather than the journey);
- Keep a paper bag in the car in case you need to breathe into it;

- Advise your travelling companions of how they can help – do you want them to talk to you or stay quiet? Are they ready to pass the mints?

### Whilst driving:
- Eat or drink something cold – have mints, an apple or water easily at hand;
- Turn the music on and sing;
- When stopped in traffic, move your legs, arms, face and shoulders to keep them relaxed rather than clenched and tense;
- Take in your surroundings;
- Turn off the road if you need to;
- Get out of the car and walk around a little to dissipate the energy of the attack and calm yourself enough to continue with your journey;
- When the feelings subside (and they will), keep driving if you can, or ask a companion to take over;
- Celebrate your success – note how far you've come, both literally and mentally and feel proud of it.

### Can you say goodbye to panic attacks forever?
Absolutely. You have to, and you must. The challenge with panic attacks is that once you've had one, or several, it's hard to forget and shift the thought from the back of your mind that one day they might come back. But you can't allow that to dictate what you do or how you live your life, or it will start to shut you down.

As we've looked at here, there's a lot you can do from a practical point of view to ward off a panic attack and ensure that it doesn't start. And even if it does start, there's still a lot you can do to manage that process. It doesn't have to be the full kick in the chest every time. So please be confident that whenever this happens, however your stress manifests itself, you can manage it, and you will.

The best way of all to deal with it is to keep your life calm and as free from stress as possible.

## Success story

*Melanie's story: from nervous wreck to confident driver*
Melanie, who took the slow road, says:

'I think I'm a success story. I grew up in London so had no need of a car. Then I moved to the country, had lots of lessons, and passed my driving test aged 32.

Then my husband got a company car, I drove it and panicked in a car park, and hit a pillar. After that I used to feel sick every time I got behind the wheel, but I persevered.

Going anywhere new (even 100 yards up a new road) felt like a major adventure. But gradually, I built up my repertoire of roads/routes/places I could cope with. Apart from dual carriageways and motorways.

Then we moved to where we live now. The supermarket is just off the dual carriageway, but also reachable the long way round, on ordinary roads. My first visit, I went the long way. It involved a very long, very steep and twisting road up a hill, which I hated. On the way back I just bit the bullet and went on the bloody dual carriageway. The road was empty. It took ten minutes to get home. Job done!

Now, I drive every day without a second thought. So, my advice is – take it slowly. Drive alone if possible. Keep within, and gradually expand, your comfort zone.'

# 7. Therapy: what to expect and how it can help

For many of you, the practical tips given in previous chapters combined with your own perseverance will be enough to get you back out on the road. Equally, for many of you an outside, expert hand will be of benefit too. This chapter looks at how you might access that, what the options for specialist therapy are and what you might expect if you go to see a practitioner.

It is not intended to be an exhaustive list, or to recommend one branch of therapy over another. Only you can decide who'll be the best help for you, and this will depend on a number of factors including geographic location and your own personal preferences. You will also find all of the contact details for the experts quoted in this book, who are all specialists in their field, in the resources section after Chapter 8.

**Why look for expert help?**
It's very, very hard to face and overcome your fears alone. You are making life much more challenging for yourself if you try, and those people I spoke to who had worked with a therapist to help overcome their fear found the experience enormously useful.

Depending on where in the world you live, seeing a therapist may be a culturally normal and accepted thing to do, or it may be treated with some suspicion. Your doctor may be happy to refer you for state-funded treatment or (more likely) you may end up paying for these sessions yourself.

I often wonder if I had gone to see a professional, would my driving phobia have been overcome more quickly than it was. It was a very long, slow process that extended into years. But at the time I didn't even know that there were professionals that could help with this stuff. Like a lot of you, I assumed that this was a fear that I alone suffered from. The rest of the world could drive confidently, I could not.

Of course, as we now know, this is very far from reality. This is a very common fear, so much so that there is now a support industry which has grown up around it. Tap the words 'Driving Phobia cure' into an internet search engine and you will be overwhelmed with thousands of choices – home study programmes, hypnosis CDs and many, many more. So if you are looking online, be as specific as possible in your search – start by looking for some help in your local area, or nearest big town. This will help you narrow down the search.

There are a number of specialist driving confidence courses both in the UK and internationally – you'll find some of them also listed in the resources section at the back of this book.

## Where to start

Your first stop is with your own doctor, to see who they recommend. One woman I spoke to went to see her GP about driving phobia, only to find that the GP had the same fear. If you are seeing your doctor for help with panic attacks then some sort of therapy may already have been suggested.

It's very likely that you may end up funding your own therapy sessions, at least in part. But if money is the only thing that's putting you off, be aware that many training schools in NLP and Hypnotherapy offer free or reduced price sessions to help their trainees gain experience.

I went along to one of these once – the hypnotherapist talked me through a standard reframing technique. What was slightly disconcerting was that at the back of the room (out of my eye line) a number of trainee hypnotherapists were observing the session, the price I had to pay for a free consultation. And interestingly, it did have an effect – though not in the way that the therapist intended.

It was pouring with rain when I came out of the hypnotherapy session. There were plenty of parking spaces outside the clinic, but it was a good ten minute walk to the nearest bus stop. I had a leak in my right shoe. As I trudged through the rain, cold and wet, I thought – If I had driven, I'd be home and dry by now. Yet another way in which this rotten fear was making me miserable. It was a small thing, but it stayed with me and helped me to resolve to beat it.

But don't be put off by my experiences – a therapy session with a trainee is better than nothing at all. Don't be a victim and shrug your shoulders and say you can't afford it. That's simply another excuse. Talk to your doctor or therapist and see what options are available at your budget.

### To a professional, a phobia is nothing new

Remember that your therapist has heard it all before, and it's their job not to be judgemental. There's no need to be embarrassed about your phobia. They will have encountered lots of people like you. I spoke to many therapists from a wide range of disciplines and backgrounds in the preparation of this book, and they all said that driving phobia was one of the most common reasons why people came to see them.

Ask around for recommendations, much as you might do for a driving instructor. If you don't want to ask your friends, ask on an anonymous chat room – you'll find some listed in the resources section.

Many independent therapists now have websites to showcase their work, which will list the kind of issues they deal with, so again look for this as an indicator that they are the right person to help you.

Some therapists will agree to have a brief chat with you (either face to face or over the telephone) before you book in for a session. They need to know if they can help you, just as you do. Otherwise you'd be wasting both your time and your money, and an ethical therapist will not want this to happen. Don't bother with anyone who tries to do a hard sell on their services – a successful, experienced practitioner won't need to do this.

**Questions to ask your potential therapist**
1. How long have they been working in the field?
2. Have they helped people with driving phobia before?
3. What did they do and what was the outcome?

If you are nervous, write these questions down to help you remember. Tell them the reason why you're thinking of hiring them and what you'd like to get out of the sessions. Ask yourself before you speak to anyone – what would I want to walk away from these sessions with that would make it a really good use of my time and money?

You may be going along to cure your driving phobia, but it will help if you get even more specific than that. Do you want to be able to drive around your local neighbourhood? To be able to take your child to the park easily? To be able to drive home big bags of shopping, rather than carry by hand? Or are you looking to make longer trips by road?

Getting specific like this will do two things: first of all it will help your potential therapist ascertain whether they can help you achieve this goal. And secondly, it will start to convince you that you can do it too. Since every action starts with a thought, if you can imagine it, then one day you can do it. And convincing yourself is the first step.

Above all, listen to your gut instinct and look out for some sort of rapport with any potential therapist. Do you feel like you could really talk to this person? You may well feel slightly anxious when you first talk to them, since you're addressing a deep-rooted fear, so what do they do to put you at your ease?

Remember that you don't need to make a decision straight away, or work with the first therapist you speak to. If they don't feel like the right person for you, move on and find someone who does.

But at the same time, don't let the fear put you down. Don't let fear of what the treatment might involve put you off talking to someone who might be able to help.

Be aware of when you are making excuses, such as 'it's too expensive', 'I haven't got the time' etc. There will always be plenty of reasons not to get help. Getting help means acknowledging out loud that you have a problem, and not everybody wants to do this.

But remember that this isn't just anybody that you're acknowledging your fears to – it's a skilled professional whose job is to help. A therapist's job is not to judge, it's to help you using their professional skills. They are an objective outsider with a duty of confidentiality, so anything you say will not go beyond the walls of their consulting room. It won't get back to your mother, your friends or your spouse. No one will know the depth of your fears or how much you've cried. The therapy room is a supportive space to help you move forward.

## Some of the therapeutic options for dealing with driving phobia

Therapist Phil Parker is a leading personal development expert with a background in Neuro Linguistic programming (NLP) and hypnosis. This is his advice:

'The most useful people for this are those who deal in "brief" or "targeted" therapy. That means their job is to help you as quickly as possible with the issue that you want to resolve, so it doesn't involve lots of soul searching or digging through your past, just a sensible approach to making the future and specifically driving lesson/tests better and easier for you. The major recommended approaches are Neuro Linguistic programming (NLP), the Lightning Process, Hypnotherapy and EFT (Emotional Freedom Technique).'

Psychotherapist Dr David Kraft feels that it can be particularly beneficial to have driving lessons at the same time as therapy sessions, as some trips can be practised under hypnosis before you drive them for real. In his experience, some people have been able to drive again after five or six therapy sessions, whilst for others this has extended to five or six months.

## Cognitive Behavioural Therapy (CBT)

Cognitive Behavioural Therapy is a psychotherapeutic approach more commonly known as CBT, which can be best summed up as a talking therapy. By talking about what you think (cognitive) and what you do (behavioural), your therapist can help you examine how this might contribute to how you're feeling now, and what you might do to change. It is widely used in groups and one to one sessions to help people experiencing a range of mental health difficulties which affect how they feel and how they behave.

CBT practitioners help people to identify and then change their extreme thinking and unhelpful behaviour, so in a session focusing on driving you might expect on to talk about what sort of thought processes are going on in your mind when you drive, or think about driving.

This type of therapy is focused on what's happening here and now and much less so on what has happened in the past, so you would not typically expect to spend much time analysing your past life in these sessions. It is also characterised by homework, where you might have something to do in between sessions in order to put into practice whatever you've learned in the talking part of the therapy session.

So depending on what you're currently comfortable with, your therapist will set targets designed to gradually stretch your comfort zone. For example, if you can currently drive only short distances, you might be asked to drive a little further. Or if you're not currently getting into a car at all, you might be challenged to sit in a stationary car for a set number of minutes, and repeat this until you feel calm doing it. You would then go back and discuss how you got on with this homework in the next session.

The advantage of this approach is that it's very practical; goal orientated and designed to move you forward faster than you would go by yourself.

*Amelia's story*
Amelia says she has (more or less) overcome her driving phobia and has CBT to thank for it:

'When our boys were toddlers, I became very depressed, suffered terrible anxiety and in the end my GP suggested a course of CBT.

The CBT was aimed specifically at my other anxieties, and was not in any way "prescribed" for my driving phobia. It was only when filling in the therapist's questionnaires about fears that stop you doing things that I really properly thought about the driving. When I ticked the "I always avoid doing something that scares me" I realised why I didn't drive. I discussed it only briefly with my therapist and got on with coping with my other issues.

About a year later, when I was back on more of an even keel, my therapist asked again about the driving. She told me that it could "easily" be addressed using CBT methods. I thought it was a ridiculous proposition, but agreed to a fresh course of CBT just to address the driving.

The therapy had shown me all my anxieties centre on a social responsibility issue where I am terrified of hurting others. Slowly, in the safety of our very quiet village, I plucked up the nerve to drive around the block. Then two blocks. Then to my friend's house, five minutes away. In the early days I used to drive in the village, come home, then walk the route I had just driven to check for dead bodies (really!). I would also drive with the windows open. I did that for months, even in the winter so that I could hear whether I was accidentally killing people that I had failed to see.

Over time, when nothing bad happened, I stopped retracing my steps. I started driving a bit further every time. I had a strict CBT inspired timetable and I felt real guilty if I didn't stick to it – driving every other day – and it was the biggest thing in my life.

I now drive most days. It no longer terrifies me – I see it as a necessary evil now. It's getting better all the time. I'm now 34 and finally feel like a real grown up.'

What a difference a good therapist and personal determination can make.

*Megan's story*

Megan also found CBT very helpful. She lives in the Scottish Borders, where driving is essential for her to get to work.

'For about three years, I avoided one particular road which just further reinforced my fear. A new job meant I would have to travel it daily. At first, I took an alternative route on a dangerous unclassified road. I knew this was silly but the more I took the alternative route (adding miles and time onto every journey), the more my fear was reinforced. I realised I would have to break this, as winter was on the way and there was no way I could travel unclassified roads in the snow and ice. Also, the fear was peaking, and I was having trouble with every journey and beginning to crumble – ready to throw the towel in and rip up my license!

My GP referred me to a psychologist for Cognitive Behavioural Therapy. The sessions gave me tools to break the habit of using alternative, unsuitable routes. I now travel the "scary" route 90% of the time. I push myself not to give up, as I know if I do, I would have to give up my job, my future, my freedom – everything really. Many people will commend me for keeping going. It's more necessity than anything else – but I am glad to have that necessity.'

I have great admiration for Megan who grapples with her fears every day, because, really, what's the alternative? To stay confined to the house? To give in to the fear and give up her job? Good for her for accepting help and refusing to be beaten.

### Solution Focus Hypnotherapy (also known as Solution Focused Brief Therapy or Brief Therapy)

As the name suggests, this type of therapy is about looking towards the solution rather than the problem. As such it is similar to CBT in that it is much more focused on your present and future rather than the past.

Penny Ling (who's recovered from driving phobia herself) works as a Solution Focused Hypnotherapist. She says:

'I find that it's mostly women who come to me for help with driving phobia. Men tend to come for something else, and the anxiety around driving comes out later. Most people do drive but are terrified of it.

Because we focus on solutions, this therapy involves painting a picture of what you want to achieve. A phobia generally takes three or four sessions to address, although sometimes people will need to do more work on their underlying stress levels.

In the first consultation, I will ask about the length of the time they've had this problem, and the extent to which it inhibits their life. I look at the whole picture, not just the phobia, but work and home life as well. Often there's homework at the end of the sessions, such as listening to a relaxation CD every night, or writing down a scenario of what they want to achieve.

I might then move on to confidence building, or I might take them on a visualised driving test in their mind.

For people who are very anxious I might suggest simply working on their anxiety and leaving the driving to one side for now. Often people with a fear of driving will have other areas of stress in their life.

Solution Focused and other therapists will often ask what's known as The Miracle Question: If a miracle happened and you were to wake up tomorrow without this phobia, what difference would that make to your life? The point of doing this is to picture what you want very clearly, and to help you see that it is possible to achieve it. It purposely moves you along from worrying about how you will achieve your goal of overcoming your fear, and instead invites you consider what life will be like once you have done so.'

### Neuro Linguistic Programming (NLP)

NLP techniques are often used alongside hypnotherapy. NLP looks at the relationship between what we think, what we say and what we do. So again it's addressing the thought processes which produce a fear of driving, in order to help you develop new thought processes.

Ted Moreno is a certified hypnotherapist and NLP Practitioner based in California. He's a member of the American Hypnosis Association and the Hypnotherapists Union. He says:

'Driving anxiety is the most common form of anxiety that I treat in my hypnotherapy practice. It's one of the most common phobias.

Driving phobia is a form of agoraphobia. But it's not the fear of open spaces that scares people, it's fear of loss of control. Obviously, this can seriously impact a person's ability to function on a daily basis if they need to drive to work or drive for a living, especially here in Southern California where driving is necessary to get anywhere fast.

The most important thing to realize is that even though anxiety does not feel good, it will not kill you. It is your reaction to the feeling of anxiety that can make it manageable or not. Instead of fighting anxiety, just allow it to be. Notice it, and see if you can observe it with detachment. Take deep breaths and try to remain in the present moment. Realize you have a tendency to create anxiety with your thoughts so try focusing on something else, like the environment, music, or the cars in front of you. You don't need to live with the anxiety.'
www.tedmoreno.com

## Thought Field Therapy (TFT)

TFT has come under criticism for a lack of scientific research, but its proponents claim that the bottom line is that it works.

Diane Hall is a driving instructor, Thought Field Therapist and author of *L of a way 2 Pass*. She says:

'As a driving instructor, I was continually disappointed when a perfectly capable learner failed their test due to nerves on the day rather than not being a capable driver, and also the fact that so many people contacted me wanting to learn but having a great fear of doing so. I carried out research into different methods to combat test day nerves, enable pupils to take on board information more easily, and to eliminate all the anxieties/fears/phobias that people had towards learning to drive.

The most effective method I came across was Thought Field Therapy. You can use TFT to eliminate test day nerves, rid yourself of previous traumas that affect your ability to learn to drive, such as being involved in car accidents that still haunt you, through to taking away anger, frustration, fear, panic, feeling intimidated, guilty and many other issues.

It uses acupressure points, which you activate by simply tapping them with your fingertips whilst thinking about the specific issue that you want to resolve. This process has the capability of eliminating the issue that you are thinking of, whether it be the nerves before your driving test, performing a manoeuvre that you find difficult, or even getting behind the wheel of a car.

I ask the person to think of the issue that's concerning them and to rate it on a scale of 1-10 whereas 1 is little emotion through to 10 being the worst emotion imaginable. The very first person I tried this with had an absolute terror of driving on dual carriageways. In fact, she had even cancelled the previous 3 lessons with me as I had said we would work on dual carriageways on the following lessons. I used the TFT sequence for anxiety and her anxiety started at 10; within just a few moments she said "I don't know what I was worrying about, it's only another road", after a few more minutes she said "OK, let's go do this". She then drove easily, calmly, in control, confident and happily on and off the slip roads of the dual carriageway with a huge smile on her face. This is just one of many times I've seen a huge change by just a few minutes of using TFT. The skill in using TFT is to make sure that you are tapping the sequence relevant to the emotion that you're feeling.'
www.Lofaway2pass.com

## Finding help online: home study programs

If, for whatever reason, you can't or don't want to go and see someone, but you feel like you need a professional helping hand, then there are a number of home study options available. With something as personal and perhaps embarrassing as this, the online world can be very appealing – you can reach out in anonymity and get help without really having to reveal anything of yourself.

But when you do you may find it both simultaneously easy and difficult to find help for your driving phobia online. Despite the millions of websites that pop up on search engines promising help for driving panic, these can be disappointing once you start to look into them. They tend to be stuffed with keywords to please the search engines, so the article that looks like it might be helpful often turns out to have very little to offer, and may in fact be a hook linked to an online sales program.

If you can find a good one, the advantage of these types of programs is that they're very easy to access, no matter where you live – you could download one and be using it in under five minutes. They take less time to use because you don't have to get to any therapist's office and home again. They're generally a much cheaper option than going to see someone in person. You can use it at your own pace and buy a hypnotherapy CD or audio recording and listen to it over and over again, as often as you need.

However, this can be a false economy. The disadvantage of home study programs is that it will still take plenty of effort on your part to get the benefit – it's not a magic pill. You could (and I'm sure many people do) buy the CDs and reading material and leave them sitting in a drawer and never use them. Downloading an app by itself is never enough. You're still going to have to make an effort: for example you may still have to arrange for time to yourself away from other responsibilities so that you can listen to the recording.

And above all, you're still going to have to get in the car. No substitute for that.

There's less pressure on you to make it work – no comeback if all you ever do is download the material and never use it. So if you are planning to use a home program, treat it as if you had made an appointment with a therapist. Block out time in your diary. Make space in your life to follow the program – arrange childcare or do whatever you need to do to carve out this time.

And if you are one of those people who's downloaded a home study program and not used it, take this as a sign that you might be better served going to see someone instead. It's not a failure to admit this.

You'll find a range of home study and online resources listed in the back of this book.

### Success story
*Sam's story: helped by medication*
Sam Wyld is a writer and mother of two in her late thirties who had been a confident driver for 20 years when she began to dread it. This coincided with other stresses in her life:

'My husband's health deteriorated just after the birth of our son in and I was forced to drive everywhere with all of us in the car. I was extremely tired with a newborn and would find myself having to squint to see, particularly in the dark or at dusk and I started to get a bit slower.

Then I began to notice every little dip or camber and one day, whilst travelling at 70mph on a dual carriageway I suddenly felt like the car was going off-track by itself and I felt like I was floating above the wheel, becoming detached. I was terrified to brake as the act of braking made me feel the car was toppling sideways but terrified not to as I had an urge to "give up" and let go of the wheel. This began to happen more frequently and I would feel out of control on slight bends or anything over 40mph.

I eventually went to my GP and he prescribed me Fluoxetine [an antidepressant, also known as Prozac], saying that anxiety and depression can overlap. They have definitely helped and I am much more confident on the local roads. I do need to keep a hand in though, or I'll scare myself again. I do find that's the key.'

# 8. Success stories: people who've overcome fear of driving

So we're almost at the end of our journey together now, but before you go, here's a chapter that's intended to inspire you. We're going to meet more of the people who have overcome their fear of driving to become confident drivers again. We already met some success stories like these at the end of the previous chapters, and hopefully you will have started to get a sense that although it is a big challenge to move beyond this fear of driving, it's not an impossible goal.

It's a good idea to read this chapter with your notebook at hand so you can note down anything you learn. What did other people do that you could do? Where do their stories ring bells with you? What can you see that your next step needs to be?

If you've read through the whole book before you take any action, right now you should be at the stage where a definite plan is emerging from your notes. Your instinct is probably telling you what your next step needs to be. That'll be different for every person, so write down what it is for you – what is your instinct telling you right now that you need to do when you've finished reading this book?

The crucial thought to take with you from here is: it can be done. Even a very severe driving phobia is not unbeatable. Other people have done it, so by definition it can be done. And if it can be done, then logically, you can do it too.

So let's look at:

- What has worked for other driving phobics?
- What was the turning point that helped them overcome their fears?
- What difference has this made to their lives?

## How do they do it?

People who overcome fear of driving don't have any special magical powers or resources which aren't available to you. Yes, in some cases they took driving lessons or sought professional help, but not always. Sometimes it was simply their own sheer determination that pulled them through. However they did it, they put their fear of driving in the past and became confident drivers again.

Think about some of the toughest challenges you have faced in life. Maybe you had to deal with the loss of a loved one, gave birth or faced up to illness in yourself or your family. We've all got our stuff in life to deal with, so I bet there has been at least one majorly challenging episode in your life. Something that, if you'd known about it in advance, you'd never have thought you could deal with, but you did.

Take a few moments to think about that now.

And driving? Next to that, it's nothing.

When I was struggling to get to grips with driving, I used to tell myself out loud: I have given birth to two children; I have watched loved ones die; I have faced enormously stressful situations. I dealt with it all and survived, so I can do this. Or more often, it would boil down into a single mantra to be repeated: I can do this, I can do this.

So remember: you can do this.

Sometimes when you do the thing that you fear most, in the process you discover that it's nowhere near as bad as you thought.

## Meet the success stories

As you read this chapter, remember that all of us are just like you. When it comes to fear of driving, we've been where you've been. We've had the panic attacks, felt the shame and misery of it all. If we can do it, so can you. It may take more courage than you think you have, an iron will and grim determination, but you can get there.

All of this is possible – I even heard of one man who over-came a fear of driving to become a taxi driver, and a driving instructor who recovered from a fear of motorways.

*Deborah's story: a tale of determination*

Deborah Riccio finds driving tough, but still manages to do it every day:

'I didn't think I needed "help" until about a fortnight after the second crash. I'd taken a week off work and during this time, I drove my daughter to school in the next village and then came home. I'd sit in the drive, in the car for at least half an hour before I got out, just rigid with realisa-tion that I'd driven at all.

Eventually I changed my working hours, so now I start work at 9.30 and leave the house when the roads are less busy. Sleeping tablets also helped enormously. I'm a very light sleeper, so the fact I'd take a tablet and slip dream-lessly into sleep and not wake until morning was such a comfort. A restful night goes a long way to feeling better the next day. I also had counselling sessions for about five months.

Now I drive to work and I drive home. I'm still rigid in the car. I don't ever relax, sometimes I can't even have the radio on in case the noise subdues something I need to react to. I need to be alert constantly.'

I think it's inspiring that even though driving is still a source of stress for Deborah, she doesn't give up.

*Olivia's story: helped by driving lessons*

Olivia found that the right driving instructor, plus her husband keeping his comments to himself, have helped restore her driving confidence:

> 'I felt terribly embarrassed and ashamed that I didn't drive especially as I had a license. I booked a lesson with an instructor who took me somewhere very quiet and we started slowly. I had a few lessons in his car then a couple in ours, at which point he said I didn't need any more and to get going with it! He gave me a lot of confidence and in hindsight my original instructor only taught me how to pass a test rather than how to actually drive.
>
> I was particularly scared of "meeting situations" like roundabouts and junctions but I feel so much more in control of the car now it isn't really an issue. I now drive myself to work every day and feel like it's such an achievement. My husband is banned from commenting – he's realised his "helping" actually does the opposite.'

*Vic's story: hates driving but does it anyway*

Vic hates driving with such a passion. And yet he doesn't give in to the fact that he doesn't like it. He's a success story against the odds.

> 'I passed my test on my ninth attempt. Strangely I knew I would pass my test eventually as a psychic had told me when I was 15 I would have a driving job, I am still waiting for that one!
>
> I don't like driving far, it tires me a lot and then I panic that I will lose concentration, although motorway driving doesn't bother me. NO to SNOW – the mere thought sends shivers down my spine. I hate driving and I can't wait to never have to drive again.'

That's OK Vic. Liking driving is not compulsory, though refusing to be beaten by it is.

### Sophie's story: a happy driver again

Journalist Sophie Atherton found that her fear of driving started after a bereavement but happily she has managed to overcome her fear:

> 'I'd been a perfectly happy driver before then and am again now, but for a while it was an ordeal. I did still go on long journeys but once had to stop and book into a hotel because I was afraid to continue.
>
> I also remember I was particularly terrified of the southbound stretch of the M5 motorway between Junctions 19 and 20. I recall driving down it with two passengers and demanding that they talk to me, incessantly and about anything, to take my mind off it as I had this totally irrational fear that my car would somehow flip over and fall onto the northbound carriageway below.'

Sophie was able to overcome her fear without any outside help:

> 'I kept driving even though I was afraid and then one day noticed that I was enjoying it again. The sun was shining and I'd got some music on in the car and I was zipping up the M4 to London and it felt great. I was so glad to be over the fear as learning to drive at the relatively late age of 25 gave me so much more independence that I'd hate to have to do without my car now.'

### Ellie's story: doing it for the kids

Ellie found that family commitments were what it took to face her nerves and get driving:

'I was petrified of driving at first but passed my test first go. I still don't like it but I do it because I have to. The main bulk of my driving is within the smallish town where I live so I am fine there; I know all the routes well! A good friend of mine can't drive, she is too nervous and relies on lifts from everyone. While I can definitely understand how she feels there is a part of me that thinks it's a bit selfish not to at least try, especially when I see her kids arriving to school drenched to the skin.'

## The benefits of fighting fear of driving

As we've heard in all our success stories, the benefits of overcoming fear of driving go far beyond reclaiming the ability to jump in a vehicle and go from A to B.

Maybe you'll take a job or a holiday that you couldn't have considered before. You'll have the choice of whether to see friends and family more often and strengthen those relationships.

You'll become a positive role model to others by showing that you can overcome a fear. And to your children you already are a role model, so grasp the opportunity to be a positive one rather than a victim of fear.

There'll be less stress on whoever does the driving right now. Until you start driving you may not realise that it can be quite tiring at times. So if your partner is currently doing all the family driving, they'll appreciate it if that load can be shared.

But above all, you'll benefit from being back in control of your life rather than having your life decisions ruled by fear. You'll be in the driving seat both literally and metaphorically.

*Poppy's story: minimising both car size and anxiety levels*
Poppy's another fan of sat navs to ease driving anxiety:

'When we got a bigger car, that's when I got more nervous. I felt sick and would shake so much in the car I'd have to stop. In fact, sometimes I had to leave an hour or so early because I'd feel myself starting to get so worked up. My husband was brilliant, really positive and encouraging but it's tricky to drive when your legs are shaking!

However, we bought a smaller car for me to drive around in about a year and half ago. I drive it to work every day and now I'm pretty confident. A sat nav and a good look at Google Maps satellite images is usually enough to get me on the road. I will leave really early to give me loads of time to get there and to park, but I can travel relatively stress free. I avoid things that make me anxious. So I try to drive outside of busy times, try not to drive at night or in bad weather and choose where I park carefully. I leave early so I can park further away and still have time to walk to my destination. So not ideal, but I can at least pick up my freecycle items!'

## My story

In my case, I would say it was sheer determination, plus driving lessons, that got me back out on the road and past this fear after seven years of not driving. I still feel very happy and mentally high five myself when I have a successful drive.

I recently went to the supermarket with my kids, a journey which involved navigating several big, busy roads I hadn't driven down before. So I got there, all fine, and as we stopped in the parking spot I breathed a big sigh of relief, gave myself a round of applause and let out a 'Woo! Go me! Good driving!'. My daughter rolled her eyes with all the world weariness an eleven year old can muster and an unimpressed 'Oh mum, it's just driving to the supermarket – what's the big deal?'

A very big deal indeed, as it turns out.

Every new drive I do is a huge buzz. I was recently birth partner to a friend who was having her baby in a hospital about 40 minutes away via motorway. If I hadn't been able to drive, I couldn't have been the birth partner and would have been unable to support my friend when she was having her little girl.

Where possible, I still practise new routes. So I did a practice run in the weeks before the birth – drove to the hospital, parked in the car park, then turned straight round and came back home.

A few years ago I came back to my car to find that I'd parked in the wrong place and been given my first parking ticket. Far from being annoyed, I was really quite pleased because I felt that this was one of the indicators that made me a 'proper' driver again – I really was one of the club. Later I wrote about this for the *Daily Express* newspaper, under the headline 'Why my parking ticket made me so happy'. I have written for lots of newspapers and magazines in my career, but this article has drawn far and away the biggest response – so many people, strangers I had never met, got in touch to say that they had read my story and that fear of driving was something they suffered from too. So that was the first indicator to me that this was a far more widespread fear than those of us in the grip of it ever realise. And that was the start of the journey towards writing this book.

But still I don't take overcoming this phobia for granted. I see my driving confidence as a work in progress rather than a done deal. I set bigger and bigger goals – longer drives, bigger stretches of time behind the wheel. Living in a busy city and mainly working from home, my lifestyle doesn't require me to drive every day, but if a couple of weeks have gone by where I haven't driven then I get a bit antsy and am keen to get behind the wheel again. When I was building up my driving confidence and travelling for a day out with my family, I would make a point of driving at least one of the legs of the journey. Now, I don't feel I have to make such a point of doing that. If I'm choosing not to drive now, it's not through fear.

And that's the biggest issue – my decisions are not controlled by fear. As we looked at earlier in this book – it's not about the driving or even the car. It's about living under a dark shadow and having your life controlled by fear.

That's no life for anybody, and certainly not you. You deserve better. Step away from the dark shadow. Life is better in the light.

Go and sit in your car right now and say 'I can do this'.

Because deep down, you know you can.

## Be your own success story

Take a moment now to visualise yourself as a confident driver. Read through this section, and the success stories at the end of each chapter again, then close your eyes and do it.

Imagine yourself in your car, about to set off on a journey you're looking forward to.

Here are some mantras to take with you out on the road:

- I am a safe and confident driver;
- Calm and confident;
- Calm, calm, calm;
- I am enjoying driving (force yourself to smile).

Of course these will feel a bit false at first – you might be saying that you feel calm and confident, though your legs may be wobbling and your arms feel like jelly. But what's the alternative? Do you really think it would be better for you to say 'This is scaring the life out of me?' The whole point of using these mantras and saying them out loud is to convince yourself so that eventually you believe it. We all get more of what we focus on in life, so if you focus on calm then you will achieve more of it. Focus on where you're headed, even if you haven't quite got there yet.

And even if you have read this far and aren't ready to take any action yet, at least take with you the knowledge that you can do it. Knowledge is power, and you have that power now. Whether you need extra professional help or not, one way or another you can do this. If you are living with fear of driving, what you are living with is a very, very common fear that few people admit to, but which ripples through every society where there are cars. But it's a fear, it's not a life sentence. You can beat it.

You can do it.

You can become a confident driver.

Now, when will you start?

# Useful contacts and other resources

**Experts**

Thank you to the experts who have shared their advice. Here's how to get in contact if you would like further support. Please do get in touch – they will be happy to hear from you:

Tracy Dempsey – Coach
www.soulambition.co.uk

Barbara Ford-Hammond – Hypnotherapist
www.barbaraford-hammond.com

Diane Hall – Driving instructor & Thought Field Therapist
www.lofaway2pass.com

Dominic Knight – Clinical hypnotherapist and NLP Master Practitioner
www.dominicknight.co.uk

Dr David Kraft – Psychotherapist & hypnotherapist
www.londonhypnotherapyuk.com

Charles Linden – Anxiety Expert
www.charles-linden.com

Penny Ling – Solution Focused Hypnotherapist:
www.pennyling.co.uk

Ted Moreno – Hypnotherapist
www.tedmoreno.com

Dr Carina Norris – Registered Nutritionist
www.carinanorris.co.uk

Dr Rick Norris – Chartered Psychologist and Visiting
Consultant at the Manor Hospital Walsall
www.mindhealthdevelopment.co.uk

Phil Parker DO Dip E Hyp P NLP MBIH, Certified Master
Practitioner of NLP
www.philparker.org

Mike Rees – Drive Alive UK Ltd
www.drivealive.co.uk

Dan Roberts – Cognitive Therapist
www.danroberts.com

Peter Skelton – Driving Instructor
www.peterskelton.co.uk

Julian Smith – Ride Drive
www.driving-phobia.co.uk

Sharon Stiles – Hypnotherapist
www.sharonstiles.co.uk

Liz Williams – Complementary Therapist
www.orchid-therapies.co.uk

## Professional associations and organisations

*AA (Automobile Association)*
The AA (Automobile Association) offers a free two hour Drive Confidence course in the UK (www.theaa.com/driving-school/index.html)

*Anxiety UK*
Anxiety UK is a national registered charity for those affected by anxiety disorders. Provides support via an extensive range of services (www.anxietyuk.org.uk)
Tel 08444 775 774

*Association for Solution Focused Hypnotherapists* (www.afsfh.co.uk) has a database of UK Solution Focused Hypnotherapists.

*British Association for Behavioural & Cognitive Psychotherapies* (www.babcp.com) includes a section where you can search for officially accredited Cognitive Behavioural Therapists in the UK and Ireland in your area. Includes the option to search under specialism so you can seek out a therapist with experience in helping people with phobias.

*British Society of Clinical and Academic Hypnosis* (www.bscah.com) includes a register of approved practitioners who offer clinical hypnosis.

*Driver and Vehicle Licensing Agency (DVLA)*
(www.dft.gov.uk/dvla)

## Online anonymous discussion forums
www.fearofdrivingforum.com
www.driving-phobia.co.uk/phobic-drivers-forum.htm
www.nomorepanic.co.uk/forum/

## CDs/downloads
Available from Amazon, iTunes or direct from the author:

*Unlimited Confidence* CD – Phil Parker
*Meditations for Manifesting* CD – Dr Wayne Dyer
*Overcome Fear of Driving* CD – Darren Marks
*Hypnosis CD for Fear of Driving* – Sharon Shinwell
*Pass Your Driving Test With Ease* MP3 download – Marisa Peer
*Self Hypnosis – Fear of Driving* MP3 download – Rachael Eccles
*Pass Your Driving Test/Driving Nerves* (two track CD) – Glenn Harrold
*Free meditation download,* – www.themeditationpodcast.com (iPod not required)
*Guided meditations* to download – www.MediatationOasis.com
Charles Linden's *Panic Attack Eliminator App* is available from itunes here: http://itunes.apple.com/us/app/panic-attack-eliminator/id380995697?mt=8


## Books
*Dû- unlock your full potential with a word* – Phil Parker
*Feel the fear and do it anyway* – Susan Jeffers
*L of a Way 2 pass* – Diane Hall
*Think Yourself Happy – The simple six step programme to change your life from within* – Dr Rick Norris
*Healthy Eating* – Carina Norris
*You Are What You Eat: The Meal Planner That Will Change Your Life* – Carina Norris
*The Girl's Car Handbook: Everything you need to know about life on the road* – Maria McCarthy
*Car Smarts: An Easy-to-use Guide to Understanding Your Car and Communicating with Your Mechanic* – Mary Jackson
*Positive Under Pressure: How to be calm and effective when the heat is on* – Gael Lindenfield & Malcolm Vandenburg
*Super Confidence: Simple steps to build self-assurance* – Gael Lindenfield
*Boost Your Confidence with NLP* – Ian McDermott (book and CD)

**Personal stories**

Thank you very much to the people who have shared their driving stories for this book. Some opted to be anonymous and their names have been changed at their request. Thank you to:

Sophie Atherton – www.SophieAtherton.co.uk
Kate Brian – www.katebrian.co.uk
Babar Coughlan
Molly Forbes – www.mothersalwaysright.wordpress.com
Lucy Jolin – www.lucyjolin.co.uk
Judith Morgan – www.judithmorgan.com
Alison Percival
Deborah Riccio – www.chicklittings.blogspot.com and the
    www.strictlywriting.blogspot.com
Nicky Taylor
Sam Wyld – www.wyldflower.co.uk

Thank you also to the posters from Mumsnet.com and Netmums.com who shared their driving stories with us.

To contact the author visit www.JoannetheCoach.com or email info@joannemallon.com or on Twitter @joannemallon

# Index

adrenaline 93
agoraphobia 12, 122
alcohol 59
amaxophobia 9
amygdala 93
anxiety 33–4, 61, 66, 73, 74, 76, 89–111, 124
armed forces 25
aromatherapy 49–50
autoautophobia 9
autophobia 9

baby, having a 10, 11, 17, 18
belief in yourself 13; *see also* confidence; positivity
benefits of driving 38; *see also* driving for fun
blood sugar levels 59–61; *see also* diet, importance of; nutrition
body language 45
breathing exercises 56, 96, 98, 99
bridges, fear of 30–1, 34
Brief Therapy *see* Solution Focus Hypnotherapy

caffeine 59, 101–2
car crash, experience of 10, 11, 42, 64

car manual 67–8
claustrophobia 12, 28
Cognitive Behavioural Therapy (CBT) 118–21
comedies *see* laughter; positivity
confidence 14, 24-5, 62–3, 70–1, 75, 84–6

destress 47-8, 54–5, 64; *see also* breathing exercises; relaxation exercises
diary 47, 63, 70
diet, importance of 59–61, 100–1, 103, 108
distraction 73, 94, 103, 105–6, 107–8
driving for fun 38-9, 41–2
driving goals 69
driving lessons 36, 42, 65, 76–81
driving phobia
    definition 7–9
    reasons 10–12
    symptoms 14–15
driving technique 39

emetophobia 12
enjoyment of driving *see* driving for fun
essential oils 49–50

exposure therapy 21
exercise 47–8, 63

hodophobia 8
home study programs 124–6
hypnotherapy 22, 72, 114, 121–2

journal writing 63, 70

laughter 52–3, 66; *see also* positivity
learned fear 13-14
learning to drive, fear of 23–5
life coaching 44, 45, 51, 62

mantras 55, 97–8, 99, 128, 135
medication 61, 126
meditation 48–9, 61
moods diary 47
motorway driving 26–7, 80
music 54–5, 66, 80, 103, 105–7

Neuro Linguistic Programming (NLP) 117–18, 122–3
nutrition 59-61, 100–3

other drivers 31-2, 39–40, 70–1

panic attacks
  cause 92–3
  dealing with 93–4
  definition 90
  stopping one 103–4
  symptoms 90–1
  whilst driving 94–8, 110
parallel parking 28–9
parent influence 10, 18–19, 41, 86
parking, fear of 28–9, 45
peripheral vision relaxation technique 57–8; *see also* visualisation techniques
positivity 52–3, 55, 66, 96, 97-8
post-trauma 11
pot plant theory 62–3

range anxiety 32–3
relaxation exercises 56–9, 64, 94, 98–100, 104; *see also* breathing exercises
reversing 33
road rage 12

sat nav systems 27, 32, 64, 82, 96, 132–3
Solution Focus Hypnotherapy 121–2
speed 83-4
stationary traffic 28

stop driving 10, 64
stress 10, 25, 43–64

tailgating 83, 84
therapy options 21, 113–26

Thought Field Therapy
    (TFT) 123–4

vertigo 12
visualisation techniques 45,
    50–2, 54, 56, 57-8

Lightning Source UK Ltd.
Milton Keynes UK
UKOW02f1314090317
296241UK00001B/8/P